from Barb Nichols — 2014

Three Gifts

Other Works by the Same Author

Books
> *Numberland*
> *Bird*
> *Quiet Answers*

Musical plays
> *Numberland*
> *Musicland*

Music and dialogue recordings
> *Numberland*
> *Numberland Music*
> *Musicland*
> *Children's Musicland*
> *Something Bright and Beautiful*
> *Bird*
> *Lessons from Bird*

Three Gifts

By

Auriel Wyndham

Mountaintop Publishing

Printed in the United States of America

ISBN 978-1-893930-05-6

Mountaintop Publishing
California, USA
www.MountaintopPublishing.com

Contents

Introducing

THE THOUGHT TREND INSTITUTE

Katie Durham paced back and forth along the driveway at the entrance to the Institute. She even walked up and down the steps towards the wide front doors a few times as though that might hasten his arrival. A steady stream of attendees for the conference had been flowing in to the small Santa Barbara airport and train station throughout the morning. Some guests had even arrived the day before and stayed overnight in local hotels. So, from various locations, the travelers were being picked up to be transported into the hills.

After fifteen minutes of winding roads their vehicles would pass through the Institute's gated entrance, then up the long drive. As they reached the top of a steep incline, an inspiring lifted white roof line, which looked almost like a sail caught in the wind, would rise into view followed by the streamlined body of the main building. Smaller structures, flanking the large one, each with their own little sail-like roofs, would then become visible. This was obviously a compound designed to delight and invite. Moreover, the utter simplicity of it all promised peace to those who entered.

However, at this point Katie was anything but peaceful. He was her assignment for the day, and she couldn't find him among the latest newcomers. She had waited in the large foyer during the registration period, but now groups were gathering for orientation tours, and one special visitor badge still lingered on the table. So at ten thirty Katie abandoned her foyer wait for the unproductive pacing of the driveway. Having watched carefully as a van deposited the last arrivals right in front of her, she became even more agitated.

"I don't understand it. He shouldn't have been hard to spot," she thought after carefully scanning the temporary name tags provided by the drivers. But no one appeared to have the name of Josh Hamilton.

Other hosts who had been appointed to escort the attendees had already claimed their groups inside, but Katie had been assigned to meet only one person, a reporter from the Associated Press, and her guest was nowhere in sight.

"Okay, so he's missed the welcome and registration period, and now he's missing the orientation tours," Katie remarked to herself. "Maybe he won't even show!"

Katie finally turned to go back inside when the sputter of an old and ailing engine caught her attention. Looking like something out of a classic movie, a rather dilapidated vehicle crawled up the driveway and came to rest almost in front of her.

The engine sighed with relief and so did Katie. Obviously, the car had done its duty and now it was her turn. She couldn't help smiling at that thought. Guessing the young man who emerged from the contraption was Josh, she stepped forward with outstretched hand.

"Are you Josh Hamilton, the reporter? I'm Katie Durham, your host for the day. I'll be showing you around and to the conference room, but you can't get the full tour at this point as it's getting late." That was as close to a reprimand for tardiness a congenial host dare give to a guest.

The young man didn't pick up on that but simply gave her a quick look and disregarded her hand, while mumbling something about losing his way. He fumbled for his suitcase and briefcase, both of which looked almost as ancient as his transportation, and then asked, "Do I park the car somewhere special?"

"Oh, no, someone will do that for you. Just leave the keys inside. It'll be quite safe here," Katie said reassuringly. "As though anyone would possibly want to take that heap of junk!" she exclaimed to herself.

As the two climbed the broad steps up to the main doors, the obviously reluctant guest remarked, "So, this is the Thought Trend Institute. Hmm, your roof lines look like sails, you know. Are they supposed to echo the sailing business carried on in

Santa Barbara? Some kind of advertisement for the area, I guess."

"Oh, no, it's not that at all. The roof line is supposed to suggest movement, like sailing down rivers of thought."

"Huh!" Josh still seemed unimpressed. "I figured the building would be very grand with an imposing marble entrance."

"Well, the research that goes on in here is probably the only imposing part. And we hope that's solid like marble, but just not as cold."

Katie had replied almost too quickly and crisply, so her companion finally took a good look at her. The first things he really noticed were her bright blue eyes, short reddish hair, and a very pink scarf used to accent a black and silver sleeveless dress. In addition to being smartly attired, she had an easy and confident manner about her. Not wanting to stare too long, Josh continued with his questions.

"So is this a type of think tank for futurists? You figure out future trends so businesses can make more money. It's a mere cog in the wheel of capitalism, right?"

"That sounds a little jaded, doesn't it? You really have no idea what goes on here, do you? How come you're attending this conference?"

Josh, obviously deciding to be more agreeable, replied in an almost friendly tone. "The guy who was supposed to cover this was sent overseas, so I'm his replacement. No, I really don't know what it's about. Had no time to research, and it didn't seem like a top priority."

"Oh, you thought that? So tell me, what topics or fields do you usually research and cover?"

"Recently, they've been giving me odds and ends, just this and that. Lately, I was on the archaeological beat."

"Aha!" Katie replied casting a look back over her shoulder at his car.

"You think that's appropriate, don't you, because I drive a relic." At this point they both laughed and a comfortable silence followed for a few moments as they entered the building. Katie quickly scooped up Josh's visitor badge as they walked straight through the main house and reception foyer to the other side and then out into a large courtyard, part of which was glassed in. The smaller buildings, some of which were visible from the outside formed an almost perfect circle around the courtyard.

"Well, this is interesting! It looks as though you have eating or meeting places right here. What do you call this space?" Josh was intrigued by the setup.

"It's our Food-for-Thought Court. You see those small rooms all glassed in? Well, we have short presentations given there at different times. We can take our food in from the serving area over there to the right and attend any meeting that catches our interest. There's going to be an introduction to that in about five minutes. It would be a good place to get your feet wet, but first I'll show you to your room in the hospitality wing."

Josh wasn't too sure about getting his feet wet, but he was on assignment and required to fit into the program. At least, he could put his suitcase down in the small bedroom that Katie ushered him into. It was nicely, but simply furnished and even had its own tiny bathroom attached. Josh thought it looked more like motor home accommodations than a "stay-for-awhile" type of place.

"I get the feeling that simplicity is the order of the day around here. You can tell by the architecture, the way the buildings are planned, and the furnishings that I can see so far." Josh had made a quick assessment.

"So you notice details. Guess that's a requirement for a good reporter. Yes, it's definitely a well-planned simplicity we have here. Isn't that what scientists and mathematicians often call the elegant solution to any problem? I mean the simple solution?"

Josh nodded his agreement. He was a tall, slender young man with rather curly brown hair which he'd been unable to tame, so he'd given up on that, figuring the natural way was the best way.

"Yes, that saying is a takeoff on Occam's razor, I believe. The simplest explanation or solution is usually the correct one. Of course, it doesn't always hold up, but it's a good place to start."

Katie was somewhat impressed. This was a thinking young man. Yes, they might just possibly get along, she thought, but said out loud, "I'm sorry you missed the welcome juice and cookies."

"That's okay. I snacked all the way up from San Juan Capistrano. "

"Well, brunch will be served at eleven soon after our little meeting. Then the first session of the conference will begin sharply at noon."

At this point the two were back in the food court, and Katie looked around and observed, "The Ethics Room is filled and so is the General Topics Room, so let's attend the Practical Bible meeting. It should be a good introduction and will attract some guests like you."

Katie was right. In fact, there were many visitors milling around as no seating was provided for this occasion.

"There must be over twenty five or thirty people squeezed in here. Are they all guests for the conference?" Josh asked.

"Most of them are," Katie answered. "But there are staff members here too who escort groups of several people. You were a last-minute addition to our list, so I don't have others to accompany."

"That's good," Josh seemed happily surprised, "so I'll have your whole attention." As Katie looked at him, he quickly added, "I may have lots of questions."

At that moment the meeting began with the ringing of a little bell. The crowd immediately quieted down and an enthusiastic woman introduced herself. She brushed back her dark brown hair, which was streaked with gray, as though she couldn't wait to get started.

"Welcome, everyone, to this food-for-thought moment. First of all, please make sure the ringer on your phones is turned off while you're here today. I'm Phyllis Graham, a presenter, and right now we'll spend only a few minutes on this subject which is titled 'Should we spring forward or fall back?' This has nothing to do with clocks, but everything to do with life and decisions. Because our subject comes under the Practical Bible, it will be tied to that."

Josh raised his eyebrows and looked at Katie who simply nodded. Explanations would obviously come later.

Phyllis continued almost breathlessly, "I just can't wait to tell you how I've had to learn moderation. It's all too easy to rush in when you have something worthwhile to do or share with others, but it's not always the best course to spring forward. Look at the disciple Peter, for instance, as he rushed to join Jesus in walking on the water. He was going to sink until Jesus rescued him. Obviously, Peter was out of his spiritual depth. But there was something else to consider and that's purpose or motive. Peter's purpose in walking on the water was undefined. He said he wanted to be sure it was Jesus, so maybe it was a kind of test, but as he started to walk on the waters he became afraid of the waves. Perhaps a better purpose would have sustained him and removed his fear, as it does with most of us.

"So, in a way it's a matter of timing, but not according to a clock. We need to do the right thing at the right time, but the right thing has to include the right purpose in doing it. What motivated Peter? Well, he was an impetuous kind of guy, so it looked as though impetuosity just took over. Oh yes, moderation is a wonderful asset. " Phyllis paused to look at her notes.

Josh chuckled and whispered to Katie, "She couldn't *wait* to tell us about her moderation?" Katie just smiled.

"But there's the other side to that," the presenter continued. "Falling or holding back could be due to fear. The children of Israel really had a rather short journey ahead of them to the Promised Land of Canaan, but they took a circuitous route due in great part to their fear. They also believed reports about the strength of the people in that region and so hung back. Falling back out of fear can put us out of our right time frame, just as surely as springing forward impetuously does.

"I've even heard it summed up this way, that the right thing at the wrong time is no longer the right thing. Maybe that's like brushing your teeth on a bus while on the way to work. Ugh! Not a pretty picture that one, but it makes a point. So, it's good to remember that we can be more effective and successful in whatever we do, if we do the right thing at the right time! Now, speaking of that, brunch will be served quite soon, so just take that hallway over there and follow it to the end."

The brief assembly was over and the guests filed out towards the dining-room wing. Josh followed Katie out and queried, "That was a food-for-thought session? It was more like a snack."

"Oh, it was simply a taste to give an idea of what goes on in there. No time for an in-depth discussion. We have to keep up with the agenda. No lagging behind," Katie said.

"Right, we can't afford to fall back." Josh seemed a tad flippant even to himself, and he wondered about it. Somehow he just wasn't taking this assignment very seriously, at least not yet.

The cafeteria style brunch was ready in the serving area for the guests to select and take into the light-filled dining room a few steps away. The well-spaced dining room tables ensured that conversations didn't intrude on each other, while the well-carpeted floors helped to mute the sounds of dining.

It was a relief to many to be immersed in a tranquil environment if only for a day. There was no ringing of cell phones or music blaring. Not even a TV in sight. As Josh sat down next to Katie he took a moment to assess his surroundings.

"Yes, this is definitely a thinking place, very peaceful and calm," was Josh's conclusion to himself as he gazed around.

What he didn't know was that in a very short space of time, in less than an hour, his thinking would be jumping through all kinds of hoops, and he would not be alone in those mental gymnastics.

Session One

Session One

WHY ARE WE ALL HERE?

The conference room was filling up quickly throughout its three sections. A slightly raised but broad platform in front of the curved seating was furnished with only a long table and some chairs. The audience would have no trouble viewing a seated panel, Josh concluded. It appeared as though the room would be packed as it was already almost full, while some attendees were still busy finding their assigned section. Katie and Josh located and entered the guest row.

Sensing Josh's questions, Katie said, "This room should be totally filled, and it holds one hundred and fifty people. Each of the three sections has fifty seats, but we can add extra chairs for special guests as needed. The acoustics are so good that we don't really need microphones, but there are some available and the panel will use them just to make sure that no one misses anything."

"Who are all these people?" Josh asked, after he had a chance to look around.

"They come from all over, but mainly from three disciplines. Wait and you'll hear soon."

At that moment, four people entered and took their places on the platform. One of the four, whose well-tanned appearance told the story of an outdoors man, called the meeting to order as he stood beside the long table in front of the audience. He had a three-member panel with him, whom he proceeded to introduce after his opening remarks.

"Welcome everyone to the Thought Trend Institute. I'm Eric Newland the Chairman of the Executive Committee. You'll agree, I'm sure, that everything begins with an idea of some kind whether it's a building such as this or the type of chair we sit on. The clothing we wear, the shoes on our feet, all had their genesis in ideas. The better or more useful the idea, then the better and more useful is usually the product of it. We here at the Institute, however, don't deal with furniture or clothing trends. The thought trends we follow are ones that will influence our world for better or for worse. It's good and more than useful to see the direction we're all taking together. Now, we welcome you to what we anticipate will be a ground-breaking meeting. Today we're going to set sail together and explore new territories of current thinking, so we hope you'll enjoy this adventure. Our panel is Julie Chin, Richard Abernathy and Elle Gillman."

Each stood and was acknowledged by the audience, and then Eric continued. "Some of you may have already been aware of our work here, while others have not. This Institute has been watching thought trends since it was established in the year 1994, but it has concentrated mostly on the theme of mankind's Ethical Development. You've probably read a bit about us on the introductory board in the foyer during your orientation tours. Someone, unfamiliar with our initial research, has already slipped me a piece of paper with a question about ethics that would be useful for all to know. So, I'd like to ask a good friend of mine, Maxwell Morgan, to come up here and address the subject for a minute or two. Max is a veteran of the Second World War and has been working for decades in the legal area of corporate ethics. He's interfaced with us on a number of occasions. Here's a mike for you, Max."

A rather spry man, obviously in his late eighties, almost bounced up to the platform and took the offered microphone and a piece of paper from Eric.

"Alright, let's see what we have here." He squinted at the paper then pulled out his glasses. "Oh it's just a basic question, nothing too complicated. Someone wants to know the difference between ethics and morals. You can find some good explanations on the web, but I find the easiest way to think of it is this. If it applies to a collective, you're usually dealing with ethics, and with an individual you're usually dealing with morals. Morals can define your own character, but ethics have more to do with a social system. Moral standards or rules are often written down in laws. For instance, Moses wrote them as the Ten Commandments. You can't steal and you can't murder are legal fixtures. Ethics on the other hand tend to develop and vary as times and situations change. And, there are different branches of ethics such as social, company or professional ethics. Does that help to clarify it?"

A woman on the left-hand side of the room raised her hand, and Max nodded towards her. "There's a problem I have with this. What if I work in a company and their ethics don't match with my moral standard? Do I leave or try to help change them?"

"That can be a knotty problem," Max answered thoughtfully. "And there will be instances where there is no obvious right or wrong. Take for instance a trial lawyer who knows his client is guilty of murder. He can refuse the case but he can't change the system because legal ethics demand that the accused be given a fair trial. I think overall you just need to remember that, while your own moral code may not change, your ethics might need to be more flexible because they can be dependent on others. Yes, what the collective decides is ethical for certain situations may not agree with your own individual moral standard. And you may need to make an allowance for that as part of the democratic process. And strange to say, a large corporation, for example, may be unethical but not illegal, so there are often no quick fixes to certain situations.

"Now, I'd like to make the point that ethics are so necessary in today's world, though of course the ancients debated ethics. Socrates, Plato and St. Augustine all had views and wrote on the subject. But since the 1970's, the department of applied ethics has taken shape. Yes, applied to business, science and technology. Perhaps the technology and inventions of recent years have given it new impetus and importance, but definitely the deep consideration of ethics is here to stay." Max handed the microphone back to Eric, and just as energetically as he had stepped up, he stepped back down and took his seat, while Eric turned to the audience.

"Thank you, Max. Now, a few years ago, we added a new branch of inquiry to our ethics research. The Institute was given a generous grant to watch for an area titled The Practical Bible. In other words, to take note of how the Bible is being made practical in everyday life. In this way, the Bible would be lifted out of a system that only religion has owned, and be regarded as a resource for all thinkers. Now, I think that just about does it, so Julie would you take over please?"

The audience, especially on the right-hand side of the podium, broke into some whispered conversation among themselves as Julie Chin moved forward.

"We have invited you all here today to consider a question which is closely aligned with The Practical Bible. 'Why is it that the churches are diminishing?'

We have three different fields represented to consider this topic. There are attendees here from the religious community in the first section to my left. There is also a medical group in the middle section of the room and finally those from the field of science are in the section to my right. Now, I must begin with an admission. We had to persuade and cajole some of you to come because you didn't think the topic was germane to your field, but we hope to prove otherwise. As this is a conference, you're all invited to participate as we go along. You're probably aware that a special morning meeting will be held tomorrow, but it's geared towards the religious section. However, if anyone else from the other two sections would like to sign up for that too, you are definitely welcome.

"Back to today's meeting, there are microphones available and the ushers spread out across the room will get them to you quickly. And, oh, uh do feel free to call out for a word definition if you need it. Even for a simple word as it helps clarify things. We always do a lot of dictionary work here at the Institute."

"Thank you, Julie," Eric resumed. "Yes, you may ask questions or make comments during this discussion, but please confine them to only a few minutes long and keep them of general interest."

He'd hardly finished that statement when someone called out a question. "Is this some kind of holistic conference on mind, soul and body?"

Eric looked startled and replied, "Not really, but why do you ask that?"

"Well, because the sciences appeal to the mind, religion tries to save men's souls, and the medical concentrates on the body. So there you have science, religion and medicine. That's mind, soul and body, isn't it?"

"Quite a surprising bit of addition you've done there, and in a way it does apply. Yes, uh, we hadn't considered this meeting holistic though I suppose in a way it is. Holistic meetings usually consider the individual as a whole. We'll be considering society as a whole and not as unrelated parts. Yes, there will be interconnectedness discussed. So, you're already adding to our adventure. Your comments here today may even take us in directions we hadn't planned, but that'll only make it more interesting. Now, as I was going to say, I'll be moderating the meeting and Richard Abernathy will start us off."

Richard stood, picked up a microphone from the table and looked out at the audience. He had a military bearing, with gray hair and a mustache. His clipped British tones could easily be heard all over the room as he began with a startling statement.

"The question posed today is a large one indeed. Why is it that the churches, even the mainline churches, are diminishing in attendance and membership? Yes, a large question, but I'm going to suggest that it can be answered in one or two sentences and by this audience no less."

The audience was taken by surprise and erupted into whispered conversations around the room.

"Yes, yes, I know you're wondering how that could be, but just bear with me for a minute or two. Let's start by asking someone in the medical community a question. Perhaps someone quite experienced in administration? Do I have a volunteer? And please introduce yourself."

After a long moment of silence a woman stood up. "I'm Megan Reynolds and I'm a supervisor in a large hospital in the LA area." Her strong voice needed no amplification.

"Thank you, Megan, for volunteering. Now, the question is this: Would you say that this period of time in our country is mainly a religious, a medical or a scientific one?"

"Well, they are all obviously present. The medical system is well established and you can find deep pockets of religion in this country such as the Bible Belt. But if you're asking which one overall is more prominent right now, I'd have to say it is science."

"That was a quick answer. So, audience, do you all agree? May I have a show of hands? Is this a scientific age we're in right now?"

Hands went up all over the room, so Richard continued. "Well, there seems to be good support for Megan's analysis. But may I ask how you could answer so quickly, Megan? Have you already thought about this?"

Megan, who had just sat down, stood up again but this time accepted a proffered microphone. "Well, yes, I have, and it began with a chance meeting I had with a couple, a husband and wife, in 1982 in San Diego. I was a young nurse in the ER at the time, and they told me that the times were changing. They said that some time back we had a religious era and then a medical era. When I asked what they meant, they said we were transitioning from the medical era of doctors and lawyers and that soon the medical field would be overtaken by a scientific period with scientists and economists. As I thought about it, I told them I felt it was already happening. I've never forgotten that conversation."

"That's fascinating. Why did they pair doctors with lawyers and scientists with economists, do you know?"

"They were researching thought trends. I suppose it was a bit like what you're doing here at the Institute, except it was just the two of them. They came up with the idea that each period contained a binary system, in other words, a pair. For instance, in countries where religion predominated it was usually the monarch or the state that was paired with religion and sometimes governed it. And that's about all I remember." Megan sat down again, while Richard stood there looking amazed. But then so were the panel and the audience.

"I'm rather stunned. Yes, maybe we are arriving too quickly." Richard seemed almost adrift. "This is going into areas that I, we, hadn't anticipated. Oh, but we're grateful for your contribution. Um, let me just confer a moment with my colleagues here."

The panel and moderator covered their microphones and talked animatedly for a few moments before Richard resumed as lead.

"We'd like to address Megan's comments a little later on, as she has in a way shortcut our conclusions and added to them. We obviously have a group of thinkers here, so I'll continue with another question. What was it like for instance in this country during the 1700's and the 1800's? What predominated then? Would you say it was religion, or medicine or science?"

There was some discussion among the attendees at this point, until someone from the religious community raised her hand. Richard motioned for her to stand.

"I'm Candice Brewster, co-pastor of a local Christian church and, from what I've studied of religion and history, I'd say that era was quite religious, not scientific. The medical field was gaining a stronger voice, but was still evolving as the doctor with the traditional little black bag visited households. Mostly religious matters and views held people's attention. Let's not forget that the Pilgrims were religiously motivated immigrants and the strict religious views of the Puritans also helped settle this country. Those rugged individuals didn't indulge in food fads, but they certainly had a lot of moral fiber in their daily diet. Yes, the period was strongly religious and moral. We can recognize it also by the christenings. Names given to children born in those days were indicative of a religious era. For instance, girls were given virtue names such as Faith, Hope, Chastity, Temperance, Patience, Prudence, Honor, Charity and Grace. And both sexes were given Biblical names."

"Just a minute," a male voice from the back of the room interrupted. "Weren't there any virtue names for boys?"

Candice was nonplussed, so looked at Richard who in turn asked the audience the same question. At that point someone suggested the name of Braveheart.

"That's not a virtue name. That was a movie," another replied. So after some laughter the question was still unanswered.

"Well, no one can seem to think of any at the moment. Sorry about that, gentlemen. Can you think of any Candice?"

"Well, uh, not off the top of my head, but there were names like Clement that originated from virtues. Clement is from the Latin meaning mild and merciful. It just appears that the female names are more directly linked to the virtues, which in their turn were linked to a religious period. Back to your original question about those times, and taking a number of things into account such as the church being the center of the community, I feel that all of the 1700's and the 1800's in this country were strongly religious. "

"Thank you Pastor Brewster, and a religious leader of the late 1800's would agree with you by referring to their time as, 'this revolutionary religious period.' But no one today would categorize our time now as a revolutionary religious period would they?"

Richard's question was actually rhetorical, but the audience answered it anyway with many calling out, "no" and "hardly."

Suddenly there was a lull almost like the quiet before the storm. The silence didn't last very long however, for the storm arrived quite suddenly and in full force.

ARE WE OUT OF OUR ERA?

Like gale winds whipping around, an excited participant almost screamed, "Are you suggesting then that the churches are diminishing and will eventually fail because they are, in fact, out of their era?"

"I'm not saying it. You are!" Richard reassured the yeller. "Yes, you've answered the question for yourself and quite quickly, I might add. But there may also be another part to the equation."

"Now, just a minute here," an agitated member of the religious group stood up without introducing himself. "Aren't you forgetting something? What about the large non-denominational congregations? Look at how they are growing. Why, some have thousands of attendees every week. Religion is by no means dead or dying out as you are implying."

Elle Gillman replied to that outburst. "Oh, we are not implying anything at all. We have simply been watching thought trends and ask you to do this with us without any prejudice or preformed opinions. We are attempting to read the signs of the times. That's all!"

Someone in the science section chimed in, "Well, if we are going to be impartial observers we will have to admit that those large non-denominational churches are growing mostly due to the exodus out of the mainline churches, so what you have is just a shifting congregation. That's not real growth at all. You just don't want to admit the churches are in trouble."

Eric took over again at that point. "Well, if there's any doubt here today that the numbers in churches are shrinking around the world all you have to do is research it. We did and found articles such as the one by the Reverend William Coats of the Episcopal Church. He wrote about the dramatic loss of members over the last thirty five years. He made a few points regarding the decline, one being that due to falling birth rates the churches were no longer replenishing themselves. It's an interesting article. There were also worldwide studies done by the National Council of Churches. Yes, we found statistics from various sources. If that hadn't been the case we wouldn't be holding a meeting today."

"Are you going to give us some statistics?" was the next question which brought about a quick reply.

"No, we're not. Our attendees today are more than equipped to do their own research if statistics are important to you. And there are many examples you can find if you look around."

"Like the Mass Mob, the one in New York that attended Mass at a Catholic Church," Richard contributed.

"What was that about, Richard?" Eric asked.

"It was a crowd of people using social media to pick a church with very few attendants, and they chose one that could hold eight hundred people, but now had only about fifty attendees, as I recall. They swelled the congregation just for one Sunday to boost morale and the collection plate. They do it here and there it seems, and it's quite amazing, isn't it!"

"Yes, it sure is. And I'm certain you can find examples like that all over the place," Eric said.

"There are churches that hold a traditional service, and later a contemporary one." Julie remarked. "But I've read reports that show mixed results. That idea often ended up just splitting the congregation."

Eric agreed, "Yes, it's been a real challenge for churches to adjust to the times. Some church members have even admitted to putting their buildings on a type of life support, but it's extremely costly to keep them running. Now, we should move on with this discussion as our committee has some insights that may startle you, but if someone else from the religious section, with longtime experience, would like to make an additional comment, we'll entertain that first."

An elderly man arose slowly and motioned for a microphone. He clutched it firmly and stood steadily. "I'm Noel Jasper and have just turned 93, and I've retired as pastor of my church after 60 years of service."

The audience, all three sections of it, broke into a generous applause. Then Noel continued. "I've seen much change over these many years. I've prayed a lot and asked for enlightenment as to what was going on in our world, including my own church. Jesus Christ told us to read the signs of the times, and I've tried to do that. And you're on the right track here with watching thought trends, because Jesus obviously meant that. He told his listeners they could read the skies and weather, but chided them for their lack of true vision.

"So, here is how it appears to me right now. Yes, congregations are diminishing and the denominational churches are losing members to the large non-denominational ones. Studies on the subject have shown that. But there are also many small non-denominational churches being formed. It appears to be the new trend to have no designation by denomination, and perhaps that is due to the fact this is not a religious period. It could even be a good thing in one way if the doctrinal barriers between churches are being taken down. Like the Berlin Wall they haven't promoted unity but actually separated brethren.

"But there are so many facets to this subject of church membership. People are not being attracted to religion these days perhaps because it is a scientific era, which leans much on research, knowledge and demonstration. Moreover, no one wants to be preached to or at. They'd rather discuss issues among themselves or on Internet chat rooms. It's a rather talky era, and it has been ever since the 70's, a time when the talk shows became popular on television.

"People certainly don't want to hear fire and brimstone sermons or that they are going to hell for their sins. In fact, many people no longer believe there is a physical hell. It's more of a mental hell which they can face even here on earth. And I for one can tell you I've experienced hell on earth and heaven on earth too, for that matter. And that's the problem. One church woman I know, who was sharing the traditional concepts of God at a retirement home, mourned over the fact that her audience of seniors didn't believe in hell anymore, so they didn't fear the consequences of wrongdoing.

"Yes, our preaching has been mostly to do with the punishment attached to sin or for not believing in God. Fear, or the customs of the times, is what usually attracted people to the church, not love for God. And true there was much dogma involved. It's understandable why so many who don't want any more accusations, threats, rituals and dogma have opted for spirituality. This has at least offered them some hope in goodness. Oh, it may be sheer human goodness without recognition of a divine source, but it gives some rest to the weary souls in today's world. Those are the un-churched ones. But let's look now at the large congregations.

"Something is going on in those huge non-denominational churches which could only be described as a type of social contract. They often preach, if you can call it that, a kinder more man-oriented gospel on how we can achieve success and feel good about ourselves. In a way they are life coaches, and that's not a bad thing at all. Those preachers are applying a type of balm to a humanity damaged by this hectic society. You'll find their churches have many departments and committees aimed at helping their brothers and sisters, plus anyone else who asks for that matter. Their outreach extends all the way from missionary work abroad to local food pantries, from help with tax preparation to child rearing. They are communities all on their own." Noel cleared his throat. "May I continue for a minute or two? And if so, may I have a glass of water, please?"

Eric quickly agreed. "Pastor Noel we would be honored to have you continue for a couple of minutes. I believe you've earned that privilege. A short round of applause from the audience confirmed Eric's statement.

A staff member quickly produced a small plastic bottle of water and, after a sip and a short pause, Noel continued. "I don't want you to think I'm bent on giving a sermon, but this next point is very important, I believe. When he was asked which commandment in the law was the greatest one, Jesus summed it up this way. The great and first commandment was to love God, not fear or even just respect, but to love God with all your heart and soul and mind. The second was absolutely like the first, and that was to love your neighbor as yourself.

"Now, the large non-denominational churches appear to be undertaking the demonstration of the second one, to love their neighbors, and are doing this with great vigor and even with determination. It's a laudable activity. We might call them Second Commandment churches and in this way they have departed, to some degree, from the dogma and rituals of the former churches which promoted fear, not love of God as the First Commandment. Yes, the emphasis is now on helping humanity. There is a danger to this however."

Pastor Noel paused and looked slowly around. This was a man evidently used to holding his audience. He knew when and how to pause for effect, and to ascertain if he had everyone's attention. Only then did he continue.

"For instance, how many people think of religion when they hear the name of the Salvation Army? Not many, I believe.

"The Salvation Army emerged from the desire to be more relevant to humanity's needs. It came forth from the Methodist Church which had in its turn done the same thing when it became a gentler form of religion than its predecessor of Calvinism. But if this trend continues with the large or small churches today, and they do not balance the

Second Commandment's humanity with the First Commandment's imperative to love God, they might become merely new Salvation Army outposts. Oh, yes, caring and considerate but not thought of as religious by the general population. Their activities will, like their churches, be undesignated. Not merely non-dogmatic or even non-doctrinal, but undesignated as to their commitment to God. People will be attracted to them for humanitarian purposes but not necessarily for a better connection to our heavenly Parent."

Pastor Noel paused again for only a slight moment, but it was just long enough for an eager young member of the religious section to call out, "So, how do we maintain that balance of the two Commandments?"

"Well, son," the pastor replied to the young man, "that's a mighty large question, and one I've wrestled with for some time now. It doesn't make sense to many thinkers today to believe there is a Supreme Being whom we declare is not only loving but Love itself, and who at the same time puts His children into a fiery eternal time-out for wrong behavior. That doesn't stack up anymore. Obviously, we are out of step with the Biblical texts. We've misread or misinterpreted them somehow. Our God today is only one step higher than the God of Calvin who predestined some to be saved and the rest to be damned."

The pastor took another sip of water and summed up. "As I've listened to this discussion so far about the changing times, it has really struck me that understanding this is a most important point, as it does account in very large part for diminishing church memberships. In fact, I became aware of a pattern of decline as far back as the 1950's. It's totally obvious now. I'm certain this all had to do with the change in eras, and we just didn't know it. However, as Richard suggested, there may be another part to the equation.

"The world craves good news, and so books that comfort are often bestsellers. Take for instance the 'Chicken Soup' books. Because the term gospel can mean good news, we need to find out what that really is. I finally had to simply preach the gospel of love as I understood it. I couldn't do the other anymore. Yes, the good news is what we all crave. To share that will require a better explanation of the God we are to love with all our heart and soul and mind. As our understanding and love for God increases, we can share that alongside our growing love and sympathy for mankind. Then there will be a balance. I don't know what shape or form the church will take in future if that is done, or even if there will be a traditional organization, but church in the broader sense could still be a vital force in our communities. That's about all I have to say on that subject, and I thank you for allowing me to say it."

There were a few cheers but mostly a buzz of concerned conversation following this from the religious section of the room, while the medical on the other hand seemed more intrigued with the pastor's speech. However, there was only scattered interest in the science section, until someone from that group posed a question.

"Well, I'd like to know if Pastor Noel and other churches are really in step with the times. How about using the new technology and getting up to date?"

"Just a minute, please. Our church has already pursued that possibility." Pastor Candice was on her feet again. "Our membership took up the question: What can the churches do to be more relevant in these technological times? We made a lot of changes in approach by installing media devices such as huge TV monitors and a new sound system for more up-to-date music. We changed the arrangement of pews and so forth, but I kept getting the uncomfortable feeling that we were simply rearranging the deck chairs on the Titanic. No real difference has been noticed and no new swell in attendance. So, technology isn't the answer at all."

"Julie, you and your committee looked into that area too didn't you, when you prepared for this meeting? Would you like to share something on it?"

"Yes, I would, thank you, Eric," Julie said as she stepped forward. "Richard mentioned about looking at only one side of the equation, so first let me give you an equation to solve. However, it's not a number but a word equation. Context minus x plus n equals what?"

The audience seemed a little taken aback at the sudden math and paused until light dawned and a couple of people called out simultaneously, "content."

"Yes," Julie replied, looking very pleased. "There are two words that can give us a big clue as to what is transpiring today with the churches. The words are content and context. You'll notice there is only one letter different in both words but what a world apart they are in meaning. It seems that when things aren't working well in any situation, even in a business setting, that so much thought is given to context. I mean the circumstances or surroundings become all important. This might include rearranging or redoing offices and presenting a new face to the world. But what about the content of what is being presented? It's like renovating a failing restaurant, but not changing the menu. Pastor Noel talked about the need to review the content when he suggested getting a better explanation or view of God. Now, recent authors on the subject have suggested simply changing the methodology and not the message. But that's not what we have found. You see, in order to be true to our mission, we studied thought trends in the Bible.

"Our committee noted that people's ideas of God changed considerably over time. In the early part of the Old Testament the Jewish nation thought of God as a rather warlike, vengeful, tribal and even changeable deity called Jehovah. This view of God transitioned in the Psalms of David to a kinder, more constant, compassionate deity who was ready to aid and protect, as a shepherd would care for his flock. Think of the comfort so many have found in all kinds of situations just from the twenty-third Psalm.

"Then in the New Testament we find a view of God as unchanging love and even Love itself. It's as though the concept of God went from the physical to the moral to the spiritual level. Yes, the content or the message about God has changed radically over time, and of course the methodology along with it.

"We concluded that the context or setting shouldn't determine the content but the other way round. In other words, the subject should be central and dictate the surroundings. That would be true anywhere, in a restaurant, business or in a classroom. And of course one could give a timeless speech on a simple outdoor speakers' platform. Yes, the setting of the Gettysburg Address didn't alter the content. The subject, if it is of any real importance, should be considered as greater than the circumstances surrounding it, just as an individual is greater than his circumstances, otherwise he could never rise above them." Julie paused and motioned to a woman in the religious section. "Yes, the lady over in the second to back row, did you want to comment?"

"Hi, and yes. I'm Dee Copeland and I just have a quick comment. Have you noticed how children often love to play with a big box that a gift comes in, without paying any attention to the contents? They become enamored of the packaging. So, perhaps we're like children in our spiritual development and have been paying too much attention to how a religion is packaged, and not the gift itself."

"That's an excellent point and analogy and we thank you, Dee. Actually, we did come across many congregations who have done a good job of rethinking what could be termed the packaging of the past. They showed a new freedom but found that still wasn't the issue. It may be a step though to considering the contents."

Dee replied, "So it's not the 'think outside the box' type of saying, but in this case, think inside the box."

Julie smiled in agreement. "Absolutely right, because as our committee did that, we found another interesting fact about changing views that included man's relationship to God. This relationship also made transitions. It morphed from people being lowly servant-subjects, almost victims, you could say, of their deity to humble, willing servants and finally to beloved children of God. Yes, mankind's views were undergoing a couple of radical changes all throughout the Bible."

"So, what was your final analysis Julie?" Eric asked.

"Well, our committee would have to agree with Pastor Candice, that technology isn't the answer to the decline of the churches. If there is an answer to the question about religious relevancy in this scientific period, then it will doubtless be found in content, in a greater understanding or knowledge of God as Pastor Noel has suggested."

"Thank you Julie and we'll keep those comments in mind. Now we should give a few more minutes to our discussion of eras, but first let's take a quick standing break." Eric turned to the panel and they, as well as the audience, took up his suggestion.

ALL ABOUT ERAS

Josh stretched his long legs before standing up and following Katie out into the aisle. "That was strangely interesting, and I've been taking some notes, but I really don't know where we're headed or even why I've been sent here. It's nice having a day off in Santa Barbara, but I can't figure out why this meeting is all so fired important."

"Well, to be honest, I can't tell either, at least not just yet, because I wasn't part of the Practical Bible Committee. They and the panel were given the assignment on the decline of church memberships. I've been in the Ethical Development section for some time now, and it's fascinating to see the direction our country, and the world, is taking in that area."

"I bet it is! And it's probably sliding downhill." Josh had a return of his somewhat cynical attitude, but suddenly decided to soften it with a question. "So, do you think ethics in general might possibly be improving?"

Katie paused for a thoughtful moment but before she could answer Phyllis came running by to say, "Oh, Katie do make sure our reporter meets the panel afterwards, won't you, in case he needs more information. We'd like all of this to be written up

47

accurately." And then she was off to her seat in the row behind them, so Katie turned to Josh again.

"She's usually in a bit of rush. Guess moderation isn't so easy to learn for any of us. Where were we? Oh, yes, about the ethics improving. It's really hard to say. We have such huge concerns today that involve ethics, such as cloning and stem cell research. And then there's the drug industry too. I feel as though our ethics are almost being formed as we go along, as research and inventions take place. Guess that's what Maxwell Morgan was saying. But they were right a few minutes ago. This is definitely a scientific age."

"Yup, that's very true. But something is nudging me about this era stuff. I'm still trying to figure it out. Oh, better take our seats again," Josh commented as the panel picked up their microphones.

Eric addressed the audience, "I'm sure you wonder where all of this is going. To tell you the truth, we do too. Oh, we have research and reports to share with you, but your contributions so far are actually bringing up more questions, and I'm not sure we have the answers. So, we're all explorers today. But first let's wrap up our recent discussion on the eras. Our research showed, in line with Megan's comments, that although all three systems or fields of religion, medicine and science have co-existed in this country since its inception, they took turns in being the prominent field beginning with religion. Is there agreement with our guests today on this finding? Maybe someone from the science section would give their view?"

A rather serious looking man stood up. "I'm Dan Voss, a physicist. The sciences were not very developed in this country during the 1800's, that's true. Take for instance electricity, which is so basic to all the inventions and gadgets we have today. It wasn't until 1930 that most homes in urban areas in this country had electricity while only about ten percent of the rural homesteads did. Even by 1939 only about twenty-five percent of rural homes were equipped with electric power, and that was the year the Second World War began. Not so long ago really. So, I agree with you in a general way, though you're drawing very sharp lines regarding all three systems. They were all changing or evolving together, side by side, it seems to me.

"But having said that, I'd agree the religious period was very much in evidence in the early days of this country from the 1600's through the 1800's. Yes, I agree with Pastor Brewster, and I'll add another point. The church was not only the religious center of the town but the civic center too, a place where all kinds of meetings were held. Religion was the core of their lives as the immigrants who arrived on our shores came from countries that dictated religious beliefs. The Founding Fathers forged a country which stood on the platform of religious tolerance and freedom, at least in theory. The subject was so important to them that freedom of religion is in the

First Amendment to the Constitution. The result was that in this country there is a democracy or choice of religion as well as of government.

"If you want to describe that time as a binary system as Megan was talking about, it would have to be democracy and religion, not government and religion as it is in many other countries. Yes religion was front and center during that early period. It permeated all facets of life including education. For instance, the final question on a recent Jeopardy TV program was: *The USA's oldest endowed chair is a Harvard chair of this subject, given in 1721 when that was largely what Harvard taught.* And the answer was Divinity. It was endowed by an Englishman named Hollis.

"Now, I do recall my grandparents telling me that after the early 1900's, and especially after the Second World War, many little boys growing up wanted to be doctors or lawyers. And, we have all pretty much agreed this is a scientific age, so if you want to squeeze the medical in between the two of us, between the religious and scientific periods, as you have here in your seating arrangement, I certainly won't object!" Dan finished with a flourish and smile to a round of applause and laughter from all three sections of the audience.

Eric and the panel were amused too and obviously relieved there would be no major battle over the rotation of eras. They shuffled their papers and were prepared to go on with the next subject when a hand suddenly shot up. Eric peered at the special guest row of seats and seeing Katie there asked, "Who is the guest beside you Katie? I mean the one waving his hand?"

"Oh, this is Josh Hamilton a reporter who is covering our meeting today, so he's not identified with any of the three sections. He's more or less neutral."

"Well, I've been called a lot of things in my life, but neutral isn't one of them," Josh replied as he stood to face the panel. "And I have a question or maybe an observation."

"We welcome your comments, Josh," Eric said amiably, then added, "And by the way, neutrality isn't a requirement here today though an open mind is surely helpful."

"That's good and thanks for the opportunity to participate. I just couldn't sit still because something has been bothering me, and then a huge question suddenly popped up. You see, I have a brother-in-law in the military. He's been wondering about the wars we've been fighting or trying to fight in certain parts of the world where there appears to be constant turmoil. He sees no end to it all and no good way of dealing with it either."

Richard Abernathy was quick and direct in his reply to Josh. "Well, we're glad for his service and for all our men and women in the military. I come from a military family and I served in Vietnam, so I can understand and sympathize with their frustration but what does this have to do with the discussion at hand?"

"Here's the thing that lit up like a floodlight just now when I was thinking more about the eras. Those countries that are fighting today, the ones we're involved with, are usually fighting religious wars on their own turf, isn't that true?"

"Actually, hmm, yes it is," replied Richard, "but I still don't see where you are going with this."

"That's the whole point!" Josh exclaimed with some excitement. So they're in a religious period or era, and we're in a scientific one. The two don't mesh. We are out of sync with each other. We're pushing them one way, towards democracy, and they're pushing another way to gain religious or tribal supremacy of some kind. No wonder we can't help them. We're just not on the same page, don't you see? We'd have to find common ground just to communicate with them, wouldn't we?"

Josh looked out over the audience for a glimmer of recognition as to the importance of his conclusions. However, a stunned silence of some moments followed his outburst, and then conversations erupted like small fires all around the room, so Eric finally had to call for order.

"Let's hold off on our comments for a minute and see where Josh is going with this. What are you suggesting then, Josh?" Eric asked.

"I'm suggesting that you publish a paper on today's findings and present it to the military. In fact, if you don't, I'll write about it myself in my report on this meeting and get it out into the news. I'll take it to the people."

"Now, now, don't get your dander up, young man," Richard retorted. "We haven't even had time to digest what you just said, let alone decide what to do about it."

Josh immediately regretted his implied threat, and apologized in a backhanded manner. "It just seems so important to get this information out. It really is, but I guess I sprang forward a bit too quickly with my comments. Phyllis will understand that."

Phyllis nodded from her seat behind Josh and Katie. She even patted him sympathetically on the shoulder as he sat down, while those who had heard her presentation in the Food-for-Thought Court were the only ones who understood in the least what Josh was admitting to.

Eric overlooked the reference to Phyllis and calmed the waters. "Yes, Josh, it was an extremely important observation you made and one which we should definitely consider. And we will, I promise. To understand and read our times is what we're all about at the Institute, and I believe we just saw that in action and from a guest. We must be doing something right. So, shall we all move on now?"

"Wait up a minute, Eric," Richard intervened. "Right off the top of my head there are other applications to what Josh just said, but first of all let's look at the last really successful war. I mean one with an obvious conclusion or end to it. That was the Second World War when freedom was the subject, not democracy, not religion, not vested interests or fear of communism. Every war after the Second World War has been indistinct in its purpose for this country and inconclusive in result. So, I agree with Josh, that it's vital for the military to understand the era and interests of a warring nation.

"However, there are other large implications when considering different parts of the world and our diplomatic ties abroad. Yes, there's trade and humanitarian help we give to other countries. We need to know their compelling interests and needs and so figuring out their prevailing system or era would be a tremendous boost to all of that. For instance," he addressed Josh, "where do you think Africa fits into this picture? What period is it in? Which of the three systems predominates there?"

Now it was Josh's turn to feel a little taken aback, and even put on the spot. "Well, let me think a minute."

"Yes, a moment to think is helpful, isn't it?" Richard was not out for revenge but he was not above teaching a lesson.

"Sure is. Huh! Guess I'd have to say, given Africa's needs, they are probably in the medical era. There are huge health concerns on that continent, which are being tackled and need to be if they're to gain a strong economic basis and future. Religion does not appear to be a cohesive factor, though terrorism is often waged by religious groups. Africa is definitely not in the scientific age. I haven't heard of an attempt by any of the fifty-four African nations to put a man on the moon, for instance."

"I'd agree with that." Richard was pleased with the reply.

Evidently Eric was too, for he said, "That's really good thinking and thank you, Josh! Yes, we need to explore that whole area much more deeply. Oh, did the gentleman in the middle section want to add something? And please take that mike from the usher."

"Yes, I'd like to add a comment. My name is Ted Lampson and I just realized an incredible fact. The whole world has been in a predominantly religious era ever since human history began. Even prehistoric cave drawings have been found that suggested worship of Mother Nature or animals. It's only been in recent history, since this country was settled that the other two systems became obvious and the eras rotated. First medicine and then science, with its many inventions, took center stage. It just hit me that we, especially our parents and grandparents, have seen the changing of eras. Humanity for centuries, actually from time immemorial, never experienced that phenomenon. No, they never did! I'm not religious but am sure glad I'm here today."

"Thank you, Ted, and what an overview you've given us! That could be worth a whole conference by itself. Oh, just a moment, the members of the panel are murmuring something behind me."

Eric paused to confer with the others in an animated fashion, then he spoke again.

"We're reaching a hasty conclusion here it seems, and we'll have to review it again later, but the current consensus is that the reason this country spearheaded the change in eras, as Ted has just suggested, was due to the fact it was founded on religious freedom, and of course democracy. But for now, let's get on with the program."

Feeling content with the outcome of his comments, Josh settled back as did most of the other attendees to wait for the startling insights they'd been promised. However, he figured it would be hard to top what they'd just heard.

Katie, on looking around, sensed a fresh anticipation in the air. "Maybe this is going to work out after all," she thought to herself.

THE THREE GIFTS

Eric turned to his panel. He paused, evidently to make a decision and then asked, "Elle, would you introduce our next topic, please?"

"Yes, I'm happy to, Eric," Elle said smilingly as she came forward. "Our research committee has been busy over many months preparing for this meeting. Just when we thought we knew the route we were taking suddenly we would be thrown a curve ball and everything would shift. Let me give you an example. It seemed straightforward to talk only about religion and theological matters when examining the decline of the church memberships, but not so. Without realizing it or naming it as such, we decided to take a more holistic approach to the question. The very first comment today brought that subject up and actually our research committee would agree. This is a holistic conference in that we're treating society as a whole.

"There's a reference book I've used for years as an aid to understanding the Bible and in it is a chapter titled, 'Science, Theology, Medicine.' I mentioned this to the committee and that set us on a new line of investigation, one of putting together all three disciplines or systems. That's why we invited representatives from those three fields today. Actually theology and religion are in the same family but they have very different meanings. Religion is a much broader category than theology."

"Definition of theology please," a voice called out.

"Oh, sure, yes I have it." Elle consulted her notes and replied, "Theology has been described as the science of God and the relation of God to the universe by A. H. Strong. He was of Puritan roots, a Baptist minister and prominent figure in the American theological arena in the 19th and 20th centuries. Webster's dictionary in the 1800's carried the same definition. Now modern dictionaries don't call it a science but simply define theology as a discourse on divinity, or the knowledge and study of God and His attributes.

"Research into the subject found one current opinion stating that theology is formed by religious beliefs and practices, but our committee is not really in agreement with that."

"I'm not either!" An unidentified voice from the medical section called out. "That would mean we couldn't find God apart from or outside of religion and that's not true. Many people have, and isn't that what Moses did at the burning bush?"

"What an astute comment, and thank you! Yes, we'd agree with that because we feel religion would more logically spring from theology, from one's concept of God. We all might like to ponder that especially when considering Jesus' religion and his theology. The two terms usually go hand in hand but are not really synonymous. However, we'll use them interchangeably for awhile. It appears that theology has more to do with one's concept or understanding of God, and religion with one's practice of that understanding." Elle then looked up from her notes and recapped the findings on eras.

"Now, the field of theology doesn't exist alone as we've discussed because alongside it are the medical and scientific fields, but the three do appear to have taken turns predominating in society. That understanding had us examine Biblical times and issues. We wondered what was going on then and if those three systems were present, not all totally apparent, but at least present. Then we came to the truly surprising part, and I'm going to ask Julie to tell you about it."

The petite and colorfully dressed Julie Chin walked to the front of the table with such a look of anticipation on her face that it was obvious she had a secret about to be shared with all. She adjusted the ornate comb in her shiny black hair, paused meaningfully and then began.

"It would be a shame if we just told you what we found, so we're going to ask you to be part of this discovery. Here's a question on Biblical history. Does anyone here, other than the religious section, remember what gifts the Magi, or Wise men, brought to the baby Jesus?"

Almost immediately, a fresh-faced young woman stood up. She appeared to be barely out of her teens. "Hi everyone, I'm Amanda Toomey, and I'm a hospital intern and hope to make a career of nursing. Now, don't get me wrong, I love my job and helping people but, . . . oh yes, thanks for the mike." She accepted the offer of a microphone but her amplified voice suddenly boomed out the rest of her statement, **"but it's so, so stressful!** Oops!" Amanda held the microphone farther back. "Guess that was too loud. Sorry 'bout that.

"So now, what was I saying? Oh yes, I've been studying the Bible lately to help with the stress of my job, but mainly because so many times patients will ask us to pray with them or for them. Most people know the 'Our Father,' I mean the Lord's Prayer. And the medical profession pretty much admits the value of prayer, even if it just calms the patient. But I've seen some fantastic results come from it too that the medical faculty can't explain, yes, even like the instantaneous remission of a disease.

"Anyway, I started off with the four Gospels and I read about the birth of Jesus. Now, that King Herod was a miserable excuse for a monarch, and he only wanted to get rid of the baby Jesus because he thought his throne might be in danger. People were saying the new king was born. I mean, right there, that idea was a real threat for Herod. He didn't want to go and worship Jesus like he told them. Talk about deceitful. Anyway, he sent off the three Wise men to find the baby because they were supposed to know so much. And they did find him by following a star. It's a marvelous story isn't it! And that's when they gave him the three gifts!" She paused, smiled and looked around with some satisfaction.

"And what were they, Amanda, the three gifts?" Julie asked patiently.

"Oh yes, the three gifts were, uh, just a minute. Well, one gift was gold, and that's very valuable of course, easy to remember because I like gold jewelry more than silver. The others had funny names. Frankincense was the one I could remember by thinking of Frank—he's my little brother—and incense. There are some really awesome aromas on the market today, did you know? Yes, a nice long soak in the hot tub with incense candles burning is sooo relaxing."

At that the audience couldn't help chuckling, and even the panel was unable to hide their smiles though Richard simply rolled his eyes, giving a rather good imitation of a skeptical judge on a TV talent show. But Amanda was oblivious to reactions around her as she was still concentrating. "And the last one rhymed with purr. I have a cat, you see, named Ginger. Um, rhymed with purr, oh it was myrrh. That's it—gold, frankincense and myrrh!"

Amanda sat down triumphantly, as though she had just won a prize on a game show. Even Richard finally looked at her admiringly, and whispered to

Eric, "Only a woman could do that. It's a talent!" Eric nodded and took charge again.

"Amanda has done a good and even entertaining job of listing the three gifts. But remember gifts are meant to be used, so let's consider three questions, but very quickly. We'll think of it as a pop quiz. I'll ask you to describe the use of each gift and its category." Eric turned to the religious section, "What was frankincense used for in Biblical times?"

Someone from that section called out, "It had a distinct place in religious ceremonies, usually to sanctify an offering to their deity. Though it was used for some medicinal purposes too, I'd still put it in the religious or theological category."

"Thank you," and Eric looked at the middle section. "Someone in the medical field, what was myrrh used for?"

Again, a quick answer came. "It has a number of medicinal properties so it was used as a medication. It must belong in the medical field."

"Good and to my right, what category did and does gold fall into?"

"It's on the periodic table of chemical elements. Its number is 79 and its symbol is au. Gold was and still is definitely in the scientific category."

"Wonderful!" Eric smiled broadly and congratulated everyone. "You've discovered an intriguing fact. Would anyone care to recap this finding?"

Absolute silence followed for a few moments and then, "This is unbelievable, just unbelievable!" That statement was made slowly and with great emphasis by a youngish man in the science section. He got to his feet and introduced himself while shaking his head in disbelief. "I'm Alex Crandall, and I'm in the Jet Propulsion Lab at Caltech. I can't get around this but, if we can believe the Bible accounts, it appears as though the baby Jesus was handed—symbolically that is—the three major fields of our time. He was given the theological or religious system, the medical field and the scientific one. What does that mean? And did he do anything with them?"

"Ah, that's the question of the day! We have arrived! On that note we'll take a fifteen minute break. There's a refreshment table in the foyer but please remember we'll be serving a special afternoon tea, a Devonshire Tea, after the second session." Eric turned to the panel, and they each filed out of the room, quickly and silently. The audience followed suit but not so silently.

Katie preceded Josh to the refreshment table where they picked up a couple of drinks. From there, she led the way around the various wings of the compound so Josh could finally receive his belated tour.

"You see, there are offices embedded into the sides of the foyer as it's the large main house. To our left as you know is the conference room in its own wing or house. To the right is the dining room and now if we walk just past that you'll see the next wing is a research center. It's much more than a library, but we usually call it that. Look at the computer stations and work tables all around the room. See the little chat areas for discussion and the large screen too for displaying various presentations. It's truly a multi-purpose room."

"Wow, quite impressive even to me and I'm used to a busy news room. The hospitality wing is on the other side of the conference room as I recall. You know, from the outside each small structure looks like a separate building, but I see they're all interconnected. Yes, I really like the layout. So, what about exploring the outside, the grounds?"

"Yes, let's go there now through the library doors," Katie replied. Both seemed relieved not to have to solve the questions that were lingering, ones which needed a strong focus and concentration. The large open spaces around the Institute aided this mental escape for they were too broad to zero in on pointed questions and meaningful answers. Katie quickly turned her attention to the landscape.

"We have acres of land here and some outbuildings too," Katie motioned towards the far hills.

"Do you keep horses?" Josh asked.

"That's an interesting question. We have a few. Do you like to ride?"

"No, not really but your chairman looks like a cowboy, in fact kind of like Gary Cooper out of the old western movies. You know, a bit weather beaten, tall and lanky and lopes around."

Katie laughed, "Yes, he does look like that and he does like to ride. So, you like old movies? I do, and some music from the 50's and 60's as well."

Yes, actually I do too. Goes with my old car and archaeology, anything ancient, right?"

Josh was finally feeling quite comfortable with Katie and enjoyed being able to laugh with her, though his mind was still running in circles regarding the conference. He wasn't totally sure of what to ask next, so he took the easy route and asked about the panel.

"I've got lots of ideas floating around, but maybe I should find out about your panel. They each seem so different."

"They are all different," Katie replied. "But they're alike in one way, being that they are all mature, experienced people. Eric is the most junior of them, probably in his early 60's. He was an aerospace engineer and retired early to devote himself to this kind of work and investigation. He said that you can go a long way in space exploration but even farther if you explore inner space and where thinking is going. He's been with the Institute since about 2004, starting with part time work here, and so have the others."

"Huh! I wouldn't have figured him for aerospace. So, how about Richard Abernathy? Was he in the British Military?"

"Yes and no. He's American but his family lived in England for some years. He attended Sandhurst Military Academy and that's why he sounds so British. Said it came from answering orders given with British accents. But he did serve as a captain with the U.S. Army in Vietnam and had other military assignments later. And our dear Julie Chin is a very artistic person and even painted those big beautiful canvases. You know, the ones with flowers in the dining room. She's a smart woman and ran the business office in a large hospital for many years. Yes, she has a lot of business savvy but is so kind and sweet too."

"So that leaves Elle Gillman?" Josh was making notes as Katie answered.

"Well, she has a varied background and lived in a number of countries. Plus she writes articles and books. She's probably the most senior member, but it's hard to pin an age on her because she likes to make people laugh and sometimes will do a little dance around the office. She had a very loving, not regimented, religious upbringing." Katie paused, looked surprised and added, "Oh, I just realized something. They represent the three systems. Oh my goodness, yes they do! Eric is from the sciences, Julie was in the medical field and Elle had the religious side."

Josh was surprised too. "Well, I guess there's only Richard to account for, but then the military is a constant through all time isn't it. That never seems to go away. It's a kind of background or wallpaper for any era."

"Yes, that's true. But maybe one day the military will become more like Star Trek where they definitely had a military setup or chain of command, but were on peaceful missions. I mean our military already takes aid to countries devastated by natural disasters, doesn't it? So possibly it could become totally like Star Trek one day."

"Yes, it could, and what an improvement all round that would be!" Josh replied emphatically.

On that hopeful note, the pair turned around and began walking back to the main house. They had just finished their drinks as they reached the patio, which was quickly becoming deserted except for three people still engaged in vigorous conversation.

"Oh, there are Kyle and Alicia. And Megan is with them." Katie was eager to introduce them to Josh, and as it turned out they were more than eager to talk with him.

"Say, Josh we really appreciated your remarks and think they were spot on! We've just been discussing them with Megan." Kyle pumped Josh's hand as he complimented him.

"Glad to meet you, Kyle and Alicia. And Megan, you really started it all off. I was actually hoping to interview you later. So you're all talking about the eras again? Do you have any more ideas?"

"Loads of ideas still running around," Megan replied. "But the main one we came up with has to do with the binary system that couple in San Diego talked with me about."

"Yes, we think the second subject, under the era plays a big part too. We're still figuring it out," Alicia was very animated. "For instance, those in the religious era are more likely to go to war. The government or monarch supports that as part of the era. At least saber rattling is usually part of governmental power display, but of course that might apply to any era."

Then Kyle quickly added, "And with a medical era predominating, and the lawyers in a supporting role, arguments are more likely to be settled by court cases."

"That's fascinating!" Katie exclaimed.

"So if the scientific era is coupled with economics then squabbles between nations are tackled by imposing monetary penalties?" Josh had hardly asked the question before the answers came tumbling from the others.

"Embargoes," Kyle stated.

"Economic sanctions," offered Megan.

"Freezing assets," Alicia added.

Kyle added one more possibility. "Richard just told us another way of handling the situation. He said to send them to Coventry. That was an English custom in his school days there. It meant basically ostracizing someone. You just don't include them or talk with them. Pretty rough, huh!"

Alicia nodded. "When he said that, it reminded me of the solution Jesus gave when someone commits an offence against you. You were supposed to tell him first in private, and if he didn't listen, then take someone else with you. If he paid no attention to the both of you then tell it to the group, the church. Finally, if that made no difference he would be treated as an outsider. It's called the Matthew Code, I think."

"That could work today, couldn't it?" Josh suggested. "I mean to exclude the offending country from any pact or big meetings. That would isolate them and probably automatically bring them economic troubles as well."

"So the solutions aren't war, but are all about money or the economy?" Katie was still amazed. "That sure holds up. Josh, you should write it up as a special piece."

Alicia agreed, "Yes, do write something on it and maybe collaborate with Richard."

Kyle joined in with, "Good idea, you threw the ball, and Richard ran with it. Anyway, if one or both of you will get the ideas down, even in short form, we can send it through our channels."

"You have channels?"

"Yes, we have an enterprise called The Good Connection. We'll talk about that later on," Kyle added. "It's almost time for the second session, and we need to talk with Eric first, so we'll see you later."

"I also have to meet up with someone, so I hope to catch up with you again later on too." Megan was off.

Josh turned to Katie. "That was a bit surprising but really interesting. Oh well, I guess we'd better get going as well, but first I want to thank you, I mean the Institute, for putting me up overnight. I don't plan to come for the morning session. It sounds as though it zeroes in more on the churches, but staying overnight will be a help because I can interview people after this meeting, and then collect my notes tonight to email in tomorrow morning."

"That's what they thought, and I'm glad you agree. We really don't have many accommodations here for overnight guests. Apart from your room, there is only one other single room and the rest are double rooms that have to share a bathroom. Kind of like a bed and breakfast. It's mostly for employees who have to stay the night here sometimes."

"Sounds like a step up from college dorms," Josh remarked. "Oh, look everyone has gone in, so let's hurry up, at a moderate pace of course."

Session Two

Session Two

BEFORE THE GIFTS

Eric spoke to his panel briefly and obtained nods from each one before he addressed the audience again.

"Welcome to our second session, but before we begin let's recap what we've done so far. In our first session we started off with an explanation of our research here, Ethical Development and The Practical Bible. Then we talked about the three systems of science, theology and medicine pertaining to three eras. The understanding that these systems take turns predominating should affect many areas, from the military to trade with other countries. The change in eras helps to answer why the churches are diminishing. The scientific field is more prominent right now in this country but not necessarily in other parts of the world. We also discussed the three gifts the Magi brought and came to the conclusion that they are related to the three systems. Guess that's about it. Does everyone agree with this recap?"

After a show of support, Eric continued. "So, basically we've figured out where we are at this point in history, but it's always useful to know how we got here, and that's why we're turning the spotlight on the past at the beginning of this second session. You may not be so interested in history, but it'll help us understand the three gifts and to see where we're going in the future. There was an evolution in thinking leading up to Jesus' time. So, this part is titled, 'Before the Gifts.' And who would like to start? How about Elle, would you begin please?"

Elle stepped to the front of the platform, but before she could raise her mike an angry voice shouted out from the science section.

"You promised this conference would apply to all our fields, and so far I've heard nothing but obvious conclusions about the three systems and then religious talk about gifts, Jesus and the Bible. So why are you wasting our time here? I have scientific experiments I could be conducting instead of listening to all this nonsense!"

Richard Abernathy immediately stood up to face the shouter, while another guest behind the angry man put his hand on the man's shoulder and rather loudly told him to be quiet and listen.

"Well, my friend, and I use that term generously," Richard addressed the shouter, "if your experiments can help you change water into wine, or if you can walk through a closed door, or if you can walk upon the waters, then I'd say your scientific experiments might be approaching the level of what Jesus did."

Eric intervened at that point. "Let's all take just a minute while I speak to the panel, because we can't rush in but need to build up gradually to all of our conclusions."

Most of the attendees seemed rather stunned at the turn of events. Josh turned to Katie and even they stared at each other wordlessly for a few moments. Then Josh made a quiet comment.

"I think I can finally see where all this is leading. They're going to show that Jesus impacted all three of the systems, the religious, the medical and the scientific. That's why they're all here."

"That would be my guess too," she whispered back. "It's pretty obvious now from what Richard just said, but I don't think he meant to spill the beans so soon."

"He just got hot under the collar. Maybe he sprang forward without thinking," Josh said smilingly. At that Katie chuckled a little, then both lapsed into an uncertain silence. The other attendees appeared to be somewhat uneasy too. It was obvious the conference had taken an unexpected turn and many were not sure they wanted to travel in that direction. It was almost a skeptical 'we'll wait-and-see' attitude that greeted the panel now.

Eric could sense this and it was reflected in his next statement. "We are all a little unsure at this point, aren't we? I mean, as to how our main topic is going to be addressed and be relevant. We can only ask for your indulgence a little while longer. We here at the Thought Trend Institute all have our own beliefs and leanings but have truly tried to be as objective as possible when looking at the subject from all angles. It's like detective work in a way. We follow the clues and see where they lead. We're giving it our best thought and hope you'll bring yours. Now, let's get on with our meeting by bringing back Elle."

Elle looked intently at all three sections of the room and began, "I know you're all sitting here still thinking that each of your fields is totally separate, but is that really how they started off? When we put all the pieces together they just may make for a surprising picture. So first, could someone give us the short version of religion as it appears in the Bible? Oh, yes, a hand is up in the religious section. Could you tell us a little of yourself, please?"

"Sure, I'm Bob van Dyke and have worked with various ministries and denominations for years to promote understanding and connection in the Christian community. I'm also on my local Interfaith Council. Rather than recount a Biblical history of wars and kingdoms, I'd like to share a theme that runs all through the Bible. Scholarship can illumine events by looking at the circumstances or the context of the event. However, scholarship may defraud us when we're examining timeless truths, which exist outside of circumstances. Julie, you'll recall, touched on this subject earlier. Understanding the underlying motivations, the thought trends, and tracing the emergence of improved thinking is always useful. That's the direction I'd like to take.

"As we know, ancient history is literally awash in gods—Egyptian, Phoenician, Roman and Greek gods. And it was within this culture of polytheism and idolatry that so much of the Old Testament takes place. However, if you trace those pagan beliefs and practices you'll find many of them drop away for the Jewish nation as the children of Israel journey towards a greater spirituality.

"Though monotheism, or the idea of just one God, was set in stone, literally and figuratively, by Moses, we find that polytheism, the idea of many gods, didn't give up the battle easily. For example, Daniel listed types of idols when he was rebuking the pride of Belshazzar, King of Babylon, and prophesying his downfall. That King believed not only in his own prowess but glorified, instead of the one true God, idols of silver, gold, brass, iron, wood and stone which of course had no ability to see, hear or know anything. Then Ezekiel, a major prophet, also strongly denounced idolatry, which is the pursuit of and reverence given to any other than the one God. He saw it as the greatest stumbling block to true worship. Sad to say, the children of Israel were often influenced by the societies in which they lived and even adopted their gods and idolatrous practices to some degree."

"Can you give examples of that please, Bob?" Elle asked.

"Well, yes. To begin with, Abraham's father, Terah, came from the other side of the flood as

Joshua said, where they served other gods. Abraham was brought out of that false worship, but when his descendants, the children of Israel were among idol worshippers in Egypt they fell under that influence. It was apparent even during the Exodus. Because Moses took so long up on Mount Sinai to receive the Commandments, the people persuaded Aaron to make them a golden calf to worship. Moses was so angry when he came down that he not only broke up the idol, but also the tablets on which he'd written the Commandments and had to do it all over again.

"Later in their history, Jezebel influenced her husband Ahab, king of North Israel, to stray from true worship and adopt false gods such as Baal. The prophet Elijah struck a heavy blow against idolatry when he proved Baal to be powerless. So Jezebel took off after Elijah threatening his life. People don't take too kindly to losing their idols, isn't that the truth! More than that, Elijah also proclaimed that the children of Israel had been taken captive and been led into Babylon due to their idol worship. Now, if my research is correct, after a period of three different exiles, it appears as though the children of Israel had been pretty thoroughly purged of their idolatrous tendencies and were no longer influenced by other surrounding nations."

"What do you take from all of that, Bob?" Elle was asking for a summary.

"Just as the ancient mariners had the North Star to sail by, it's obvious that Moses made a special alignment for mankind to live by. He pointed in the direction of only one God and the Word of God, but there are always influences we have to deal with like currents in an ocean. They can pull us off course if we're not careful. It means constantly aligning with the right direction, and that usually takes a lot of effort."

"So would you tell us about those same influences in the New Testament?" Elle asked.

"Well, the early Christians still had to deal with idol worship but in a more peripheral way as they shared their message with other cultures and nations. For instance, Paul was pretty upset when he was in Athens to find that the city was wholly given to idolatry, so in his address on Mars Hill he explained to them the unknown god they worshipped. But when John the Apostle cautioned, 'Little children, keep yourselves from idols,' it was obvious he was talking about what you hold dear to you.

"It appears that the view of what constituted an idol had changed from simply physical ones of gold, silver or wood idols to the 'idols in the heart' that Ezekiel warned about. It seems as though they finally learned that idols in the abstract were just as much idols as those carved by hand. We certainly could learn too from that today. Look at our current infatuation with money and celebrities, and then there's the media obsession with food, sex and prescription drugs. Part of the definition of idolatry is inordinate affection along with false reliance, worship and looking for benefits or guidance. That covers a lot of territory for our modern society."

"Yes, it certainly does," Elle said. "And we often lose our idols through a hard experience, don't we, just as the children of Israel did during the exile in Babylon."

"We do. And in conclusion I think the main point here is when Jesus stepped onto this earthly stage that his people, the Jewish nation, were no longer dealing with physical idols so he didn't have to battle those practices. That in turn helped prepare the way for him to teach higher, more spiritual values, as John the Baptist prophesied Jesus would do. That's one of the main themes and a very practical one that I take from my Bible study. There are other threads, of course, throughout the Bible, but I chose that one to share. "

"And we thank you for it, Bob." Elle turned to ask Eric a quiet question and then resumed. "I think we have time for me to touch just briefly on another theme that often went along with idol worship but actually was mentioned very early on in the Cain and Abel story. It's the subject of sacrificing something to a deity either to appease or to please. Abraham was willing to sacrifice his son Isaac. Perhaps he was still feeling the old influence of idol worship and child sacrifice from his youth, but he suddenly realized God didn't require that as a sign of his faith. Here again is an obvious transition of concepts, of thought trends, in the Bible. The custom of sacrifice changed over time from human and animal to solely animal sacrifice. Did you notice that progress, Bob, when doing your research on idolatry?"

"Yes, I did, but even that improvement, and especially the merchandising that went along with it, was rebuked by Jesus as he whipped the moneychangers and vendors out of the temple. They had quite a commodities trading market going on there. Gentile coins couldn't be used as they had a graven image on them so had to be exchanged for Jewish coins, giving the moneychangers a thriving business. The same was true of those who sold doves and animals for the purpose of sacrifice. Jesus said, 'Take these things hence; make not my Father's house an house of merchandise.' In addition, God obviously didn't need burnt offerings or the blood of innocent animals, and that's stated many times over in the Old and New Testaments. For instance, the prophet Micah denounced and totally discounted that kind of sacrifice. In fact, he went through the whole list of offering up children, or calves or burnt offerings, and put another in its place."

"Right, he did." Elle consulted her notes and said, "Oh yes, I have the exact quote here, 'He hath shewed thee, O man, what is good; and what doth the Lord require of thee, but to do justly, and to love mercy, and to walk humbly with thy God?' The apostles made statements like that too."

Bob quickly added, "Yes, Paul said the same thing to the Romans. 'I beseech you therefore, brethren, by the mercies of God, that ye present your bodies a living sacrifice, holy, acceptable unto God, which is your reasonable service.' So that whole idea of sacrifice certainly transitioned from dedicating or offering up other people or even animals, to Paul's plea for complete dedication of one's own life. No shirking our individual responsibility."

Elle agreed. "That dedication includes giving up false goals and ambitions too because, when you read Paul's statement in context, he is saying a living sacrifice means being spiritually rather than materially minded. There's a lot to give up and sacrifice right there. So it's not as simple a subject as it first sounds."

Elle was ready to conclude that discussion when a hand was raised.

"I'd like to add something."

"Sure, if it's quick, Josh," replied Elle.

"It was a news item the other day about a young guy high up in his company with a large salary. He was asked to cut forty-one employees, so he made up the list with his own name at the top. He gave up the job, the excessive lifestyle and most of his material possessions and went to live simply in a one-bedroom apartment. At last, he was truly happy he said, and is writing a book about it with a friend, I think."

"Yes, that's a good example of sacrificing what everyone else says is important, but doesn't make for happiness. I think we've all read accounts like that. It's encouraging to hear them and wish we had time for more, but we need to move on now. So, let's consider another field. Can anyone tell us about the early beginnings of medicine and particularly any link it had to religion or science?" Elle scanned the room. "Ah, yes, someone from the medical side."

"Hi, I'm Ian Flinders and a pre-med student as well as a history buff. The physician who mentors me asked me to attend this meeting and bring back notes. I'm sure glad he sent me and didn't come himself."

At that comment there were some nods of agreement in the audience, and it was obvious others were there in that same capacity. Elle replied with a smile, "Well, we're glad you're here too, Ian. So what's your take on the history of medicine?"

"Well, when I started to research it, I found out the Egyptians, for instance, had priest-physicians who were quite adept at handling diseases with herbs and acupuncture as well as prayer. Instruments for cataract surgery were found in Egypt, though early credit for that goes to India about eight hundred years before Jesus' time. Most ancient medical practice was mixed with rituals and worship. Yes, on the whole in the ancient world the priest-physician was more the norm."

"So the practice of medicine wasn't a single system at all?" Elle asked.

"Absolutely not, and it may surprise many people today that the art of medicine came from religious practices and was intertwined with them. For instance, there were a number of gods in Greek and Roman mythology and they had different functions. There were gods associated with many areas of life including gods of fertility, the crops and of course healing. Appeals were made to these gods for help. Apollo was designated the god of medicine and so people turned to him for healing. And Apollo had a son, a god called Aesculapius, and it is his rod with the serpent twined around it that is a symbol for medicine today. By the way, you'll find various spellings of his name if you research it. And if you follow the history of the healing arts there are gods and goddesses. The terms 'hygiene' and 'panacea' in fact came from the names of two of the daughters of Aesculapius. Those goddesses supposedly represented health and a universal remedy.

"Then there was an actual person, the Greek physician Hippocrates, born about 460 years before Jesus, and he was considered to be the father of Western medicine. What really shocked me was that the original Hippocratic Oath began with, 'I swear by Apollo the Physician and by Asclepius and by Hygieia and Panacea and by all the gods. . . '

"Yes, medicine had its roots in pagan worship and idolatry. Religion and medicine in ancient times were quite inseparable. But I read somewhere that Hippocrates tried to remove the mythological influence on medicine. Oh, yes, I remember now. Hippocrates told the people that the gods hadn't sent disease to them as punishment. That's what they'd believed. Sometimes, I think people still do believe that. At any rate, he made some separation between mystical religion and medicine. And by the way, they did revise the Hippocratic Oath for modern times, and it no longer swears by the gods or goddesses."

"So what was the form medicine took in Jesus' time?" Elle asked.

"Let's see, oh yes, the Romans who occupied Jerusalem were influenced by the Greek practice of medicine. Hippocrates may have left behind idols of wood or stone, but he introduced vegetables and minerals as medicines or drugs. So that was pretty much the medical scene at the time of Jesus, I believe."

"Thank you, Ian, and that was very helpful." Elle acknowledged the contribution. "So, it appears that out of the religious practices of the ancient world came the medical system and they were combined. Then the unity of religion and medicine was gradually dissolved as they both evolved until they became considered as separate systems in today's world.

"This brings up an interesting question. How exactly did religion and medicine become separated in more recent times? There was still a connection even in the modern world between the two wasn't there? Is there someone willing to comment on that? I see a hand. Yes, Megan?"

"I keep going back to that conversation I related to you. You know, it was the one with the couple who talked about the systems changing. Seems to me that as the period changed and another system took center stage that the previous one was detached from it like the stages of a rocket."

"How do mean that, Megan?" Elle was puzzled.

"Well, for instance as the medical system was coming into prominence beginning in the 1900's, the religiously-run hospitals began to diminish. But from earliest history, religion and medicine were united. That's why nurses in British hospitals are still called 'sisters' as a leftover from that time. But the state, instead of religious orders, began to fund hospitals, especially in this country, so the separation of religion and medicine was cemented. Then caring for each other was more of a physical necessity, rather than a Christian duty. I really don't know how else to explain it. But I have to add there are many wonderfully kind physicians and nurses out there today. I'm sure you've seen that too, Elle."

"That's very true, Megan. Compassion and kindness certainly are found in the medical profession. And now Richard is going to continue with the next leg of this journey."

"Yes, we need to explore the science field now. Now, can anyone tell us about the beginning of the sciences? Did they have a connection as medicine did with early religious practices?" Richard looked towards that section of the room and was not disappointed.

"Alchemy is an obvious connection," someone at the back of that group offered as she stood up to be acknowledged.

"Would you give us your name and occupation please?"

"I'm Kristin Turner and am in the science section, though somewhat a crossover as I work in biotechnology. And yes, there is a strong connection between science, religion and medicine, and it goes way back again to ancient times. Alchemy came from ancient Egypt where they practiced mummification and had a belief in an afterlife and immortality. Alchemy was what was called a protoscience, and it provided a platform for modern chemistry. It was actually a philosophy that eventually developed into the science of chemistry."

"What's the definition of philosophy, please?"

"Ah, I see we have an English scholar in the medical section," Richard replied. "Could you answer that, Kristin?"

"Basically philosophy is a love of wisdom and so a philosopher just means a lover of the wisdom found through reasoning and enlightenment, not through empirical methods of see, touch and feel.

No microscopes involved, in other words. Philosophy is a method of gaining enlightenment about almost any subject.

"For instance, the ancient philosophers, and there were many, debated the existence or nature of God and attempted to reason it all out. There's no proof, however, that their philosophies raised or improved the condition of mankind. But here's what I found on a website by someone named Cockren about the early alchemists. He says that those men were actually not materialists at all but were really spiritual thinkers who had, and I'm quoting, 'a vision of man made truly in the image and likeness of the One Divine Mind in its Perfection, Beauty, and Harmony.' That's quite a statement, isn't it!"

Richard replied, "It certainly is. I think that moderns often underestimate the thinking of the ancients, simply because they were ancient. But there was a yearning in so many cultures for that one perfect concept of being. I don't think we should forget that basic quest, or let it get lost in the details of their beliefs and practices. So Kristin, what was the purpose of alchemy?"

"Well, alchemy had some fantastic aims in mind, which couldn't be realized of course, such as a youth elixir and changing ordinary base metals like lead into gold. But it made some real contributions to experimental methods and lab techniques which we use today. Where the split from religion came is rather similar to where medicine separated from religion. You see, alchemy had its own set of religious beliefs and practices, containing mythology, magic and spirituality. For instance, alchemists were searching for the Philosopher's Stone, an alchemical substance thought to be capable of achieving their goals. The mystical part was dropped off as modern science adopted some of alchemy's framework and processes. As alchemy morphed into chemistry, it did contribute in a meaningful way to science, and even to medicine."

"Thank you, Kristin," Richard said. "So here again we have a strong connection between religion and science, as well as religion and medicine. Of course they have all been evolving in different degrees over the centuries. Are there any other comments on that evolution?"

"Yes, I'd like to disagree slightly with Kristin in that physics is usually considered the first of the sciences, and therefore a more natural first connection than alchemy."

"Oh, it's Alex Crandall, right?"

"Yes, and I've researched some history too and found that physics also had its roots in philosophy and in religion. It began as a study, or contemplation, of the natural world, that is, the material world and the elements that comprise it. Physics has a long history of evolving into what it is today. And in researching the connections, I found a statement saying that there is a direct link between

Christian metaphysics and the rise of science. Don't remember where that was though."

"Thank you for that addition, Alex. No, we wouldn't want to leave out physics. But you've just introduced another concept, so does anyone know what the definition of metaphysics is?"

"It's higher than physics, isn't it?" someone in the religious section called out, and Richard turned to Julie for the answer.

"Well, yes, it is. It literally means after physics. But it gradually became known as that which is above physics and it deals with subjects of a non-material or non-physical nature. It relates to what is transcendent, or a reality beyond the scope of the material senses. You're in mental territory with metaphysics. But mental territory like physical territory can vary widely, so not all metaphysics are alike. For our purposes the concept of Christian metaphysics should be considered, but perhaps later. We're going on to the next topic now, aren't we, Richard?"

"Yes, we are. So, concluding this discussion, we find that all three systems of science, theology and medicine were intertwined at one point in history, and not separate at all. We may even find in the future there is a point of convergence again. Now, before we talk about opening the gifts, there's another subject that still needs to be investigated. Eric is going to start us off in the right direction."

WHICH IS THE RIGHT DIRECTION?

Eric seemed almost relieved to tackle a new topic when he said, "And now leaving the history department, I'd like to ask a member of our research committee, David Carnegie, to come on up here and add some insights that he and Elle have been working on. One of which is particularly thought provoking. David?"

A casually dressed, rather stocky, middle-aged man with shaved shiny head, who looked as though he could be a wrestler, jogged up from the guest row of seating and took the mike Eric offered.

"Hi everyone, and don't be fooled by the Carnegie name. I don't come from money, and at this point in my life it doesn't appear as if I'm going towards money either."

The audience appreciated the joke and some even applauded.

"Hey, you're applauding that idea. Yes, actually there's a benefit to being financially neutral if you can call it that. The other David, the one in the Bible, had a wise son named Solomon who said in his Proverbs, 'give me neither riches nor poverty' and that's an excellent idea for a number of good reasons, yes, very good reasons indeed. But," and he paused meaningfully, then added quickly with a smile, "we won't be discussing them now."

As the audience chuckled a voice could be heard. "Isn't that a little like when Andre Rieu at one of his concerts told the audience that the 'Blue Danube' was the most famous waltz but they wouldn't be playing it?"

At that point, everyone had a good laugh. David was more than happy to encourage his audience to take the lighter side.

"Ah, it's good to laugh, isn't it! No wonder that Burt Bacharach song resonates with us all. Yes, 'What's it all about, Alfie?' I'm pretty sure Alfie didn't know the deep meaning of life, and maybe we here today can only skim over the surface, like water skiing. But it's better than sinking. So on that hopeful note, let's look a little deeper without getting overloaded."

"Good," a voice called out strong approval. "I'm glad to hear that, David. We all have too much information these days, just like we have too much stuff. And what do we do with excess? We either get rid of it or put it into storage never to be seen again. Or else we just live a confused, cluttered life. So, unless you give us what is meaningful and useful today," and the guest finished slowly and deliberately, "you will have played the part of accessory to excess."

That comment struck a chord which reverberated around the entire room including the panel and David too.

"Hey, well put by the gentleman down front, whoever you are," David was very serious now. "That's why we'll ask you to judge us not simply on our scholarship but on the useful ideas presented. I got lost and confused as I researched ancient beliefs and practices, reading contradictory information sometimes. Couldn't even tell at one point whether it was a mythological god or an actual person they were talking about like Hermes the Thrice Great. I was almost becoming, you could say, *hermetically* sealed by my research and left gasping for air and inspiration. Yes, I had to dig out of the information pile by going back to the ideas, or the thought trends. Then everything became clearer again. However, by the little information we've just shared, we can recognize how truly interrelated the three fields were. Now, we're ready to explore the ideas again.

"So, for a moment, please close your eyes and let's assemble ourselves together as one group around the three gifts, because they are about to be opened. Can you all see that picture?"

"Yes, I can," one member called out. "Me too," shouted another. "Okay, we're ready." This was the last reply, so David continued.

"But wait, there's a threat to each one of the gifts. And this is the surprising part. It isn't from hordes of evil doers or even governments bent on destroying the good to come. No, Jesus had gone off alone when the attack occurred. By then, he was thirty years old which, by Jewish law, signaled he was allowed to preach or teach in public. So what is about to happen? Let's open our eyes again."

The members of the audience blinked, gazed around the room and looked very puzzled, until one hand was slowly raised. David was quick to acknowledge the woman.

"Yes, the lady in purple at the back of the religious section. Would you tell us who you are please?"

As she shook her head 'no,' David invited her to stand and take a microphone. Again she shook her head. He then asked if she had something to contribute, and this time she nodded.

"So, ma'am, what is that please?" He asked the reluctant contributor the question slowly and respectfully. This time a verbal answer came forth quietly in two words only.

"The temptations."

Those in the audience, who were close enough to hear, began talking with each other and a voice could be heard asking, "Wasn't that a singing group way back when?"

"I'm sorry, I didn't quite get that. What was the answer, could someone tell me?" David didn't want to put the woman on the spot again.

"She said the temptations," someone helpfully repeated.

"Ah yes. Jesus hadn't even begun his mission and the temptations came. This often happens in human life doesn't it! Just when you're about to embark on something truly wonderful a snag or doubt will come up. Or you may be tempted to deviate from your good purpose. It's a devilish influence and that's exactly how it was described. The devil tempted him. I have a question that maybe I shouldn't ask here, but how many people today believe that the devil is an actual person with a pitchfork? Or perhaps I should just ask if any other person approached him, or was Jesus still alone when he was tempted."

"He was alone in the wilderness," was the only response to the double question and David accepted it.

"Yes, he was alone and had been for forty days and nights, and he was hungry. Now the two main accounts of this are in Matthew and Luke, and they're pretty much the same. Would someone tell us about it? Uh huh, I see a hand. Yes, Pastor Noel?"

"I'd like to begin with Paul's statement to the Hebrews about Jesus. He said, 'For we have not an high priest which cannot be touched with the feeling of our infirmities; but was in all points tempted like as we are, yet without sin.' That's important for us all."

"Why is that, Pastor Noel?"

"Well, it shows that we're not sinful because of what comes to us, you know, wrong thoughts, influences or suggestions. It's what we do with them that truly counts."

"Good point, and thank you. So, what were those temptations?"

"The first was to make stones into bread to satisfy his hunger. The second was a vision of all the kingdoms and the power Jesus could have if he would deviate from the true worship of God, and worship the devil. To me, that's world worship, worshipping the world. The third temptation was for Jesus to throw himself down from a pinnacle of the temple and prove that God would save him. Of course there's much more to it than that because the temptations were based on the challenge to Jesus himself. If you're the Son of God, you should be able to do this is how it's recorded."

"Thank you, Pastor Noel, and yes the challenge was made perhaps because Jesus had just come from being baptized by John at which time he'd heard the message, 'This is my beloved Son in whom I am well pleased.' So yes, right after hearing that heavenly approval and reassurance, immediately after knowing he was on the right path, he was challenged and tempted. But he turned each temptation away and didn't indulge any of them."

"So, what does this have to do with the three gifts? Or what does it have to do with our three fields? I just don't get it." A participant was obviously becoming impatient.

"Good, let's go there right now," David reassured the questioner and asked the interested audience. "Tell us again, what were the gifts?"

"They were gold, frankincense and myrrh."

"And they corresponded with what fields?"

"They corresponded with science, theology and medicine."

"Exactly. So the temptation to change the nature of matter, to change stones into bread, would fall where?"

"Oh, I see, I see," Amanda bubbled over with her usual enthusiasm. "That would be a bit like the alchemists trying to turn lead into gold. It would have to be in the science section. He was being tempted to use his spiritual gift to solve his own problem of hunger."

"And to have power over the world by worshipping the devil would be in the religious or theological part, wouldn't it! Jesus had strong words when answering that temptation. He said, 'Get thee behind me Satan: for it is written, Thou shalt worship the Lord thy God, and him only shalt thou serve.' Yes, that had to be in the theology department." Candice offered that piece of the puzzle.

"Sure, that's right," Bob van Dyke affirmed. And to throw yourself down to prove God would help you and that you couldn't be hurt would have to be in the medical arena. Okay, so Jesus was being tempted to misuse his abilities or spiritual powers for basically personal reasons; to feed his own hunger, to be a type of king or ruler, and an invincible super hero, preserved by divine power. And he wouldn't do it! He was being tempted in each of the three categories. Oh think about that for a minute! Each category! What a revelation that is! It's worth being here today just for this one idea."

Murmurs of consent and concern were heard around the room. David allowed a long minute for this to take place before he was prepared to speak again. However, someone else beat him to it, and with the vigor of an angry rebuttal.

"Hey, everyone, do you really think this is so earth-shattering? You'd think you'd just seen the CERN particle collider in action!" The shouter from earlier on now made his second appearance.

"You know you're getting to be a real pain in the . . . in the neck. You give scientists a bad name. There's some good stuff here. So, you want to discuss this with me? We could do a little colliding." The offer came from another strong voice in the science section.

"Okay, gentlemen, let's continue on with this in a few minutes, but first a little break would be in order." David looked very pointedly at the two men involved. Then he addressed the audience in more congenial tones, "It's time for us all to stretch a bit, and you can grab a soda from the table in the foyer if you'd like."

It was with relief most of the group stood up and walked into the aisles, while some headed straight for the refreshment table. Katie and Josh found themselves waiting in line at the table beside Amanda and Bob, who were animatedly talking.

"Shall we join in their conversation, Josh, do you think?" Katie whispered. "I'm really interested but don't want to just barge in."

"Why not! That's a reporter's skill you know. We can make barging in look like a gift to the other person." He then turned to Bob, "Hey, let me reach a couple of glasses over there for your sodas. They have ice in them already."

"That's very nice of you, and thanks. You're Josh the reporter, isn't that right?"

"Correct, and I'm very interested in this latest development and what you and Amanda just contributed. I think Katie is too."

"Oh, yes, I am." Katie was quite surprised at the ease with which they were suddenly included in the conversation as both Bob and Amanda turned to face them.

"Well, here's my take on it." Bob shared Amanda's enthusiasm. "We've been leading up to three main points so far and each one is quite astounding in its own right. Just look at the distinction between the eras. That's where your comments were so helpful, Josh. That applies to so much. Then next was the surprising idea of how the three gifts aligned with the three fields of science, theology and medicine. And now, well. . . "

"Yes, now," Amanda was quick to add "now we can really understand the significance of the three temptations. When I was researching prayer I just never got that part, but now it makes perfect sense. Jesus had to deal with the same kind of stuff we do everyday. We're always being tempted one way or another even if it's just to react to someone. But it's usually in the areas where we feel we can do the most good, the ones that mean the most to us, isn't that so, Katie?"

"Yes, it's usually our strong points that give us the most trouble one way or another. And speaking about the temptation to react, just look at the reaction a few moments ago between those two guests. I thought we were going to have a fight on our hands."

"David looks a bit like a bouncer, so he could have taken care of it in one minute flat." Josh dismissed that situation as a potential problem and asked Bob, "So tell us, where you think this is going next?"

"I think the only direction we can go now is to explore what Jesus did with the gifts, the three systems. What were his contributions and were they accepted? That should be the next question."

Bob's conclusion was accurate for, after a few more minutes, everyone was called back into the conference room to pick up where they'd left off. David with microphone in hand looked out across the audience.

"We'll be going next into the subject of opening the gifts, but first someone asked me at break how Jesus could so easily put off the temptations. Elle and I discussed this awhile back, and her Bible reference book was a great help to us. You'll find throughout the Gospels that Jesus constantly referred to listening to God for direction and instructions. You could say he had a divine GPS, a God positioning system available to him. So when he was tempted, that is, pointed in an opposite direction, he simply challenged the directions and turned that false message system off. Human nature is always offering its own bad advice."

"How did he turn it off, do you know?" Betsy was quite intrigued by the whole idea.

"From what we could gather, Elle and I felt he simply laid down the law, quite literally. Jesus replied to each temptation with 'it is written,' which meant he had the authority or Scriptural law to back him up in his refusal. And he gave the exact counter argument to each temptation. You could even look at that whole episode from a lawyer's point of view."

"So you're saying Jesus could resist the common human temptations because he had this other, higher, divine source for guidance. Is that correct?" Eric summed up.

"Yes, it is and I'm sure we'll discuss this again later, but briefly, Jesus could resist what Paul called 'the carnal mind,' which is just another way of saying a fleshly mind or the human mind which is opposed to God. He didn't rely on the human mind but on the divine Mind, which is God. He said he hadn't come to do his own will, but the will of his Father. That shows the difference between the human will and the divine will right there, and that they are two different, actually opposite, sets of directions."

"Is there anywhere else in Scripture that showed Jesus refused that kind of influence?" someone from the medical section called out.

"Yes," David replied. "There is one other place with almost the same wording that Luke had in describing the temptations. It was when Jesus said, 'Get thee behind me, Satan' to Peter who had rebuked Jesus when he foretold the trials he would go through including the crucifixion. Jesus, in turn, rebuked his disciple saying that he was concerned with the things of man not of God. Obviously Peter couldn't bear the thought that something so bad could happen to someone so good. But it was just a human reaction Peter had, and Jesus rebuked it because it wasn't in line with the divine directions he was receiving. This also shows that Jesus didn't consider Satan to be a human being. He wasn't saying that Peter the person was Satan, but that his faulty human reasoning was totally off base. It was a devilish or bad suggestion, just as the temptations had been. Perhaps we are clear enough now on the two opposing directions. So let's see where Jesus' divine GPS took him."

THE GIFTS ARE OPENED

Eric began, "Perhaps we all might agree with this conclusion. If Jesus had given in to those three temptations, the three gifts would never have been opened. His contribution to those fields would not have taken place." This statement was a good preface for the next topic, and most attendees nodded assent to it.

"I'd like to invite Julie back again because it's usually women who are so expert in choosing and giving gifts. So, Julie would you take over now please?"

"Yes, I will, and thanks Eric. I'm going to begin with an observation about the current state of gift giving and receiving. It appears to be somewhat a social phenomenon today that gifts, and even good deeds, are not always gratefully received or acknowledged. Have any of you found that to be true?"

"You can say that again! I was talking earlier about looking beyond the packaging of religion, well that's true with our own gifts too. Hard to tell if anyone has even opened them and looked inside," Dee Copeland complained. That's happened to me over and over. I've given so many gifts and never received any kind of thank you. I even had to ask if they've been received. And friends of mine have had the same experience."

"Well, you should do what I do," another woman contributed. "I just send a check, and when it's cashed I know they've got it. Don't know why I keep doing this, but I can't seem to stop myself. It's my way of showing love is all I can think. Maybe folks have too much today, and the gift doesn't mean a lot to them, or else they just feel entitled."

At that Dee, obviously still feeling a little irritated, replied, "And those same people expect to be appreciated. Well, you reap what you sow and that means if you don't believe in appreciating others, then you won't be appreciated either. That's the way it goes."

"In some cultures, it's a common practice to re-gift items without even unwrapping them," Dave added.

"Oh dear, but gratitude is so important," was a quiet comment from the medical section. "It would make life sweeter, oh so much sweeter, if a good deed could be noticed, and a little heartfelt 'thank you' added. I heard about a university study the other day. It was on happiness, and the very first requirement to being happy was gratitude."

"Is it the era do you think, and maybe the religious era was more grateful?" Candice asked this question. "You have to go outside of yourself to notice a gift and be grateful, and prayer does that. Takes you higher, yes, outside of yourself."

"It's just the extreme busyness of this era. Here's what I think about that," and Alex Crandall put in the proverbial two cents. "It's like a relay race today. You have run your lap, and you catch up to the runner on your team to hand over the baton, and they have already started to run. You make sure they grasp the baton, or gift, in their hand and they just keep running to the finish line without ever looking back. That's it, isn't it! Or I could put it into rocket terms by having the first booster fall off as the next one takes over without any thank you, but that image may not be as appealing to this audience."

Applause, laughter and obvious agreement swept over the room. Then Elle spoke.

"We received an email awhile ago from Brian B. in Boulder. He's a good thinker and a supporter of the Institute and this is his take on the problem. Oh, it's in the form of an equation."

"What is it with you people and equations?" An irritated voice was heard.

"Oh, we haven't even begun with math yet," Elle replied with a smile.

"Oh, great! So what is this amazing equation?"

Elle, still smiling, turned a page in her notes and quoted.

"Signs of the times = trend that folks aren't as conscientious, courteous, polite, grateful. . . so they go, go, go faster without looking back at the debris left behind!!!"

"Oh, that's so true," Dee chimed in. "And the debris would be the loved ones who are disappointed, even heartbroken, over what looks like cold indifference to their efforts to love."

"That's what happened to Jesus and he still kept on loving and doing good anyway. Take for instance the ten lepers Jesus healed, and only one turned back to give gratitude for the healing," remarked Candice.

"Those would be pretty good odds for our times. No, I doubt we'd get one in ten today," was the pointed comment from another guest.

"And maybe that's why Jesus told them to ask importunately in prayer, not just halfheartedly," Candice added. "It's not trying to convince God at all, but to show our own honest desire to see the good we feel God has for us. We want our eyes opened to it. Lots of times we don't appreciate something we thought we wanted. So praying importunately, which means urgently and earnestly, shows we have a real, honest and eager desire. It's a sign that we're really going to use what we're given."

"And that brings us to how Jesus used what was given him and his gratitude for it." Julie took over again as she consulted her notes for a brief moment. "Oh yes, he said he could do nothing of himself, but only what he was taught by the Father. That's in the Gospel of John. It was always the

Father to whom he gave thanks for his abilities. He was always grateful to the Giver, to God, and even before he saw the healing results. This means to me that we can't properly use the gifts given us by others or by God, unless we're grateful for them. So we've established gratitude first. Now, what were the contributions Jesus made to any of the systems? If you'll simply stand, I'll point to you for your comments. Yes, over there to the right."

"He turned the water into wine at the wedding feast," was an immediate reply. "That would fall in the science area, obviously."

"The gentleman on the aisle," Julie motioned to the guest.

"If we go by Matthew, after the temptations Jesus healed all kinds of sick people. That would be in the category of medicine. Then he gave the Sermon on the Mount, which meant he was in the theological system, but after that he healed Peter's mother of a fever and also a deranged man, which would fall under the heading of medicine again. Of course, it was a different kind of medicine." After this guest, then others, mostly from the religious sector, began standing.

"Don't forget Jesus and the disciples were in a ship, in rough seas, and he calmed the waters. Oh, and later on they were in a ship when Jesus walked on the water to them. And there was another ship adventure too. Jesus and the ship he was in were immediately at the place where they were going. It was almost as though he annulled time and space. So, there we have science again. Do you think they traveled through a wormhole in space?"

"That's quite a thought," Julie replied, "but I don't think we can investigate it right now. What are some other examples we have that Jesus contributed to all three systems? Yes, the lady in the tan sweater."

"Well, he taught little lessons in between his acts too, like 'let the dead bury their dead' which has been a huge help to me, not to get involved with what is unproductive. That would be theology again."

"How can you call that theology?" Dee asked.

"Because it shows me to go higher, in a more spiritual direction, that's why!" The answer was quick as another stood ready to contribute.

"There were lepers healed, and also the man who had the palsy let down through the roof to reach Jesus, all contributions to the field of medicine or healing, for sure!"

"And so many parables show up in most all of the gospels, and they teach spiritual lessons, so that's the area of theology then, isn't it."

"It would take us a whole day to go through and classify all Jesus did, wouldn't it?" Julie asked as she acknowledged one more participant.

"That's for sure, and we haven't even touched on the biggies in the healing department, you know, like healing the man blind from birth or raising Lazarus from the grave. Actually, he also raised the

widow's son and the young girl too. And then himself
. . ." Amanda was ready to enumerate further but
Julie motioned to her.

"You're right Amanda, and the list does go on
and on. But I'm interested that you can so easily
and even so happily recite these when you're in the
medical field. Why is that, do you think?"

"I think it's because I so want to help people
and not ignore their needs, even if it's just for
comfort. Jesus never ignored human needs in favor
of just teaching spiritual lessons to the people. He
had quite a crowd listening to him that one time,
you remember, and he wouldn't send them away
hungry in case they fainted on the way back into
town. He didn't just make some big statement like
God would sustain them, but he showed how God
would do it by multiplying the loaves and fishes.
Yes, he demonstrated what he taught. They even
had baskets of loaves and fishes left over. Do you
see what I mean? His Christianity was really
practical. It worked here in this world. I mean it
changed whatever the bad situation was and didn't
just promise some paradise or wonderful spiritual
world afterwards. It was more like heaven on earth.
I really like that and I don't see why the medical
field can't investigate more about how he did it."

"Thank you, Amanda, and I like your attitude
and your comments. So just to recap here, it appears
that Jesus passed effortlessly from system to system,
by contributing to all three areas, of science, theology

and medicine. I wonder how that would appear if someone did that in modern times. It would be quite astounding wouldn't it, to have an individual cross over with great success from system to system, and all on the same day!"

Julie herself was amazed at that mental picture, and yet she had been working on this very idea for months. Her audience was likewise deeply thoughtful. A few skeptical eyebrows were still raised, but Julie ignored them and continued.

"So, can anyone tell us the overall contribution Jesus made to the religious system? Yes, over there, the gentleman on the aisle, oh, Bob van Dyke isn't it?"

"Yes, it is, and I hope it's okay for me to give a little more input."

"Sure it is Bob. So how do you feel about Jesus' contribution to the field of religion?"

"First of all, Jesus' teachings were not at all popular with the establishment, religious or political. I guess if you had to zero in on the teachings that stand out the most they would be the Sermon on the Mount, the Lord's Prayer, and then parables like the prodigal son. As the Christian religion was really unformed at that time, it had to be Jesus' theology, the theology he taught, which incurred such resistance."

"So Bob, you're making the distinction now between theology and religion, are you?"

"Yes, I am. I've been thinking about what you said earlier and have come to the conclusion that Jesus' contribution was to theology, not religion, as the religious system of the time didn't change but people's idea of God did. Jesus put his theology, his understanding of God, into practice and that was his religion. He taught and lived wonderful lessons in love for us all. However, there were so many takes, or opinions, on what he taught that various religious practices sprang up. A woman I know wondered, as a child growing up, why there were four different Christian churches on the four corners of the main intersection of her tiny town. Weren't they all supposed to be Christian? That really summed it up for me. Pastor Noel said it. Man-made doctrines and creeds have actually separated, not united Christians. But as for making an indelible imprint on the world, well, obviously Jesus did that. Let me ask a question of the audience here if I may."

"Sure go ahead, Bob," Julie replied.

"Okay, everyone, here's a hard question for you. What year is this?"

The attendees seemed quite startled and were almost reluctant to reply. This had to be a trick question, they reasoned. Sensing that Bob said, "No trick involved. It's just a straightforward question. What year is this?"

At that most of the audience replied with "2014," while a few still wouldn't go along with the game.

"That's quite right, and whether you replied out loud or not, you were actually saying that answer to yourself. Yes, whether you are religious, an atheist or an agnostic, you still know the year. People don't realize it but every time we write down and mention a certain year, or just think it, we're acknowledging Jesus' contribution because his life and works even changed the calendar. It's as though history had a fresh start with the Christian era."

As Bob sat down, Julie summarized, "So the conclusion is that Jesus did use that gift. Whether or not you follow his teachings, his tremendous contribution to the theological world brought about a new religion and even changed the calendar. Can we all agree on this?"

As heads nodded, Julie continued, "Fine, would you take over now please, Elle?"

"Yes, I will Julie. So, when the gift of frankincense was opened, the forgiveness and love Jesus taught and demonstrated permeated, and perfumed, the whole world with its sweet aroma. Now, we are left with two gifts, myrrh and gold. Myrrh was attached to the medical system we decided. So what finally happened to the gift of myrrh? Was there any lasting effect on the medical system when it was opened, or do you feel Jesus has been relegated, confined to only one system, to the use of only one gift?"

"Yes, I definitely believe that," a participant was quick to reply. Only his contribution to religion has been recognized. Jesus opened the gift of myrrh, or healing, and used it, but no one really wanted to acknowledge that as a viable contribution to the health field. Maybe it would have been acknowledged if his era had been medical, instead of religious. Even the early Christians eventually lost the art of spiritual healing."

"Could you give us your name please?"

"It's Stanley Hodgson and I'm a junior pastor, here taking notes for the senior pastor. Obviously, what Jesus contributed to the religious world was marvelous. But there was so much more! However, the world put him into a file marked, 'religion' and wouldn't let him out of it. And the files marked 'medicine' and 'science' contained no mention of him at all. Yet look at his healing works! It was Jesus' method that our world hasn't accepted."

"What about the churches? You were all supposed to be following Jesus' example weren't you? We haven't heard of all your great healing work!" This rebuttal came from the medical section.

"Okay, yes, the churches are partly at fault here, too. However one church in particular was formed more than a hundred years ago to bring back spiritual healing because Christianity had lost it. That church met with very good success as well as a lot of resistance from other churches and from the press too. Maybe that's one reason why the rest of us have been a bit slow on the uptake."

"You can say that again!"

"I know, but it can take awhile to realize you have lost something, let alone to believe that it's possible to recapture it. But for some decades now my church has undertaken to heal by spiritual means, and we've had some pretty good results."

Stan was not going to be dissuaded but neither was the rebuttal expert.

"That's just anecdotal evidence, not solid at all!"

This comment was followed by a quick retort from a man in the religious group.

"How anecdotal is it, if you actually see the results? About thirty years ago, a friend of mine with a gangrenous leg was completely healed by members of his Christian church. He was going to lose the leg, but instead it was healed. There are so many reports like this given today, but you won't listen to them because they're not in your field. You act as though there is competition for healing, and your way is the only way. You ought to be calling Jesus Christ the ultimate physician, and have him as a model to emulate, instead of discounting his healing work. "

"Perhaps we all need to take a deep breath," Eric suggested. "The old saying that you shouldn't discuss religion and politics is sound advice as both topics tend to be inflammatory. So let's stay clear on this one thing. We are not debating religion, or medicine or science. We're looking at thought trends and what is influencing society, and we feel this will answer questions for the churches and why they are diminishing. It will also answer questions for the other two systems, as they each have their own problems and opportunities. The cost of health care has become astronomical, and been taken up as a governmental issue. And medical mistakes and malpractice suits are far too common.

"The sciences are not exempt either. Look at the ethical issues to be solved such as cloning, stem cell research plus replicating bodily parts. Then there is genetic engineering such as genetically modified organisms in food. These are just a few examples. If we can take that deep breath and agree to reason things out, we may be able to help this world of ours."

Scattered applause followed Eric's statement and some type of tacit agreement was reached. Richard then made a suggestion.

"Let's see if there is any kind of a bridge. Let's ask if anyone here is practicing holistic medicine and taking into account mind, soul and body? Ah, we have a hand raised in the medical section." Richard pointed to the middle part of the room. "Please tell us your name."

"I'm Joseph McIntire, a practitioner of family medicine along with my wife Dorothy. We practice holistic medicine, and perhaps that's due in part to the fact we both had a religious upbringing which we don't necessarily follow to the letter, but we still have the spirit of it. Guess you'd put us in the category of spiritual more than religious.

"It's been brought up about the mysticism and religious mythology of ancient times, but to be honest we have been dispelling our own medical and scientific myths all along the way. We used to believe that thinking didn't affect the body and that's been so disproved today in the medical field that even the NIH, the National Institute of Health, is being mandated to take up that study. It was thought until just recently that DNA was unchangeable and we weren't in charge of our genetic identity. That's also been proven wrong along with the idea that brain cells don't grow after 18 years of age. It's been shown that people in their 80's and 90's can see replenishment of those cells. Yes, our boundaries, our myths, are being shattered, along with the sound barrier, all the time. It's a regular occurrence."

"So, what are you suggesting?" Eric asked.

"Well, it's already been stated at this conference that there's a need to understand and know God who is Love. I believe if that doesn't happen then religion as we know it will disappear. Oh myths may be perpetuated because people need something or someone to believe in, and for today's world the trend is to turn inward to rely on the self. But the current saying that you should look within yourself for answers doesn't explain some of the amazing results of prayer that I've seen in my practice. Both my wife and I have actually. These instances point to a higher power outside of the human experience or self."

"How or why do you think those things occur in your medical practice? " Richard asked the guest.

"I can't really answer that. Guess I could take the easy way out and say it's not my field. I'm just one voice in the medical arena but, from what I've experienced, there is more to life than just the physical side of it. There is a metaphysical one that only just now people are probing, and that's why my wife and I practice holistic medicine that takes into account mind, soul and body. We really try to steer away from drugs as a solution. I have the feeling that one day the drug industry will be put under a microscope, and we won't be pleased with what we see.

"However, I need to add another piece here, and it's that my field of holistic medicine, which was so on the cusp awhile ago, does not appear to be so groundbreaking anymore."

"Would you explain that please, Joseph?" Eric asked.

"Well, if you read the Larry Dossey book *Reinventing Medicine* he takes us through three stages and calls them eras of medicine. First was the obvious body orientation, then next is the mind-body connection, but from there he advances to non-local consciousness where mind is not enclosed in the body. It's possible with the new sciences especially quantum physics that medicine as a whole will go in that direction."

"So is there a conclusion you've reached from all of this?"

"Yes, my final point is this. The medical and scientific fields are constantly looking for new answers. So, if the religious system is willing to do the same and to discard some of its dogma and outworn, ineffective doctrines and honestly investigate their own field, their theology, they may be surprised at what they'll find and the progress they'll make. That's about it, I guess, for now. Oh, and one last comment. I hope this conference can finally address the basic issues you've been leading up to!"

"Well, Joseph is correct in that we've been leading up to the main topic, but we still have a way to go." Eric spoke to the audience again. "It's true that there does not seem to be much exploration in the religious sector, which we can only attribute to a type of party affiliation. The Christian churches seemed to vie with each other for adherents almost as though they were political parties. Perhaps all the creeds and doctrines of the churches have indeed actually separated them, not unified them under the common heading of Christian, as has been suggested. Does anyone agree with this?"

"Yes, I do." A woman spoke up but didn't rise or give her name. "I'm not going to put my name on record because I'm in the religious sector, and I have to admit I have some doubts. It makes me feel like a heretic because I'm questioning something so foundational to most Christian churches."

"What are your doubts? What is it that bothers you? Eric asked gently.

"Well, I've wondered why they had to set everything down, I mean at the Council of Nicaea in 325. I know there were conflicting opinions about Jesus and his place or nature, and whether he was the Son of God or God in the flesh. But why did one opinion have to win and be turned into a creed for everyone to believe? Then, just like our childhood clubs with secret passwords, we all had to adhere to the creed to be in the Christian club. At least that's how I've thought of it. I heard that Christian healing was lost around that time, which also makes me think that battling over the place of a leader will cause damage and loss to any cause, no matter whose opinion wins."

"Do you have a solution?" Eric inquired.

"Yes, I do. Why not take a red-letter Bible, you know with all of Jesus' sayings printed in red ink, and ask Jesus himself to tell us in his own words about his place? Tell us just who he was. If all the churches did that with an open mind, I think there would be agreement. There would be unity."

Eric immediately supported that idea. "That's a wonderful suggestion for all the churches. Now in a way, that's what we're attempting to do by looking at what Jesus actually accomplished and not simply following opinions about him. We've just discussed how he contributed to the health system, whether it was accepted or not. Now, what about the gift of gold and how was it used? Yes, the young man in the science section? Who are you, please?"

"My name is Dave Gardiner, and I'm a grad student in physics looking for work right now, and I want you to know that I don't fear honest research in any department of life."

"So, you're telling us you're pretty much unbiased, is that it, Dave?"

"Yup, that's right. I had Bible study growing up, but along with that the world was changing tremendously, so this new generation has to be more pliable. We have to adapt, that's for sure, but to what is the question. Now, it's a fact that ordinary people have had experiences that defy the laws of physics or our own logic, and yet they've happened. We hear accounts of incredible things all the time and find them fascinating, like the person falling down a cliff unharmed in what they could only describe as slow motion. So, why are we so resistant to looking at what Jesus did that also defied the laws of physics? Let's consider his track record.

"If you take the Bible accounts at face value then obviously Jesus made a huge impact on and contribution to the science field. Think of the astounding feats that Richard spoke about earlier on, and it's obvious that our scientists today can't even come close. The new autonomous car that drives and even parks itself is pretty mind boggling even to today's youth, but it's nowhere near what Jesus accomplished. No one that I know has fed a multitude with a few loaves and fishes, or walked on water, or through doors, or out of a tomb or been instantly in another location. And teleportation like 'Beam me up Scottie' is still a long way off for us, though we'll probably be able to achieve that one day.

"Jesus did all that and more a couple of thousand years ago, and without any physical means or inventions. Now we have a couple of choices. One is to discount entirely all that is written about Jesus, including the modern-day experiences people have had in these directions, or the other is to investigate. If the accounts are accurate, then it's obvious that Jesus' gold was something we don't even know about. It had more value than we can imagine. So that's the point isn't it? How did he do the things he did, and why? The gift of gold is in the scientific field, so what was the gold Jesus used? Yes, what was his science, if he had one?"

"May I interrupt here, Dave, and ask about your science, your special area of study in physics?" Richard was curious and so was the audience.

"My major area of study has been string theory, the concept of multi-dimensions. There could be as many as eleven we figure which is called M-theory. Steven Hawking thinks this is a possible candidate for the Theory of Everything, the theory that scientists are looking for to explain the universe, but others don't agree with that. At any rate, the research into other dimensions is an accepted part of science today. So, is it possible that Jesus dipped into a dimension we haven't discovered yet, and that's how he performed what look like miracles to us? His acts may be perfectly natural and not miraculous in another dimension, isn't that so?"

At that point the entire panel applauded. And part of the audience, not really knowing how to react, followed suit. The shouter, who had been sullenly quiet for some time, now raised his voice again.

"Why are you applauding? You're just like sheep! Dave doesn't know enough about physics to make a suggestion like that. And if your Jesus did know about another dimension and use it, why didn't he tell everyone about it, huh? Tell me that! Yes, tell me that!"

"Maybe he did tell us or perhaps just showed us, only we didn't listen or understand." Phyllis suddenly stood up and faced the science section. "Think about all the parables he gave us. They could be our biggest clues. I believe it was a world of thinking, a spiritual thought world, that Jesus had access to and that we don't understand. It was a spiritual not a material dimension. That's why you can't find it peering through a microscope. He never preached about going to a special geographical place called heaven, not even one for worship. He told us to worship God in spirit and in truth. And he always spoke about wrong states of mind, not wrong places to be in. It was more like Pastor Noel said that many today believe that heaven and hell are mental not physical states.

"Jesus talked about the Kingdom of God the same way. That kingdom wasn't like any on earth. We can put a pin on a map showing different earthly kingdoms, but we can't with the Kingdom of God. Jesus said you shouldn't look here or there for it, because it's in you! That has to mean we'll finally recognize it mentally and spiritually, not geographically or physically! That's where Christian metaphysics comes in, and we need to explore that territory!" With a direct look at the shouter, Phyllis sat down.

Josh was astonished at the fervor and even courage Phyllis showed. He had definitely put her in the wrong category. This was no unsure, slightly scatterbrained, middle-aged woman. She had strength of character and insight too. Even Katie was surprised, and suddenly realized her opinions of Phyllis hadn't jibbed with the reality of Phyllis. "I wonder how many other opinions of people I have, and that are all wrong," she thought to herself.

The shouter evidently didn't have any such concerns about his opinions, as his next vehement statement immediately showed. "I know where you're going with this, and why you have us all here. We're not stupid you know! Yes, I see it all now. So, we can assume that Jesus was not only an outstanding religious leader, but the ultimate physician and probably the ultimate scientist too! He made incredible contributions to all three fields. Isn't that where you're going with this? Isn't that right?"

"Well thank you for making that point," Richard replied with a calm smile. "That's a very plausible answer and a good possibility. We certainly need to consider it. You have excellent powers of deduction."

"Oh, uh, um. . .!" The shouter was almost speechless and utterly exasperated. He made a great show of standing up, angrily looking around, and slowly and very deliberately walking out of the room and the building. He was last seen by those peering out of the conference room windows as he roamed around trying to find transportation.

One attendee sitting near a window remarked on that to the audience saying, "He could use some teleportation right now, I think. Maybe he just hasn't said the magic words."

"Beam me up, Scottie," a number of voices called out in unison and the whole audience erupted into laughter.

"What a perfect time for our afternoon break and that Devonshire Tea we've been promised, don't you agree?" The audience applauded Eric's suggestion and laughed again as he added, "And maybe someone could go and rescue that poor fella out there. He looks totally lost."

Devonshire Tea

Devonshire Tea

COME TO TEA FOR GOODNESS' SAKE!

The spacious dining room had been transformed from simply welcoming into simply festive. Multi-colored flowers in colorful vases on each table accented and imitated the flowers in the large paintings that adorned most of the walls. White, purple and pink were the dominant colors with splashes of vibrant greens. Even the table napkins complemented both the flower arrangements and the English crockery provided for the occasion. Josh remembered, as he looked around at the walls, that Julie Chin had produced those lovely works of art, and he concluded that she possessed great ability and artistry. He noted too that simplicity didn't require austerity.

Guests had been handed seating assignments as they entered the dining room and were still finding their places as Eric picked up his cordless microphone to address the group.

"You'll find all the tables clearly numbered in order beginning at this end of the room. Your place shouldn't be too hard to find. And in case you're wondering why Devonshire Tea, well, we just wanted this day to be special and different. Both

Richard and Elle have had personal experience with English customs, so they planned this for us. I'm going to ask Elle to explain it all.

Elle took over the microphone and waited for a few more guests to be seated, then began. "I hope you're all comfortable and ready for our Devonshire Tea. It comes complete with cucumber, watercress, and other kinds of sandwiches, without the crusts of course. And the famous scones will be brought warm to each table. To eat the scones authentically, just split them in half and apply a generous amount of butter to each half. Devonshire teas usually omit the butter, but Cornwall doesn't, so we'll go with Cornwall on that. Then add the strawberry jam. No other kind of jam will do, by the way, and top that with our clotted not whipped cream. Clotted is when the cream rises naturally to the top of the milk in clots. There you have it and oh, you should take milk in your tea, too."

"Do we have to raise our pinky finger when drinking tea to be authentic?" a woman called out.

"No, you don't, and in fact that might even be considered by some to be a tad affected," Elle smiled. "At least, that's what I've heard." She gave the microphone back to Eric and joined several others at her table.

Next, Eric stepped into the middle of the dining room, joined by the two guest speakers. "You'll notice a change has been made in that each table is mixed. You'll find some from the sciences, from medicine, and religion all at the same table. Added to that, our guest speakers will be mingling with you by walking around your tables with their cordless mikes while you're waiting to be served. This will give you an opportunity to participate. Now, I'll introduce our two teatime speakers, Kyle and Alicia Winston. You should know a little about some of the folks we interact with on a regular basis, and what their contribution is." Eric turned to the couple and made sure their cordless mikes were on. He then found his own assigned table.

"We'd like to begin by telling you a little of ourselves," Alicia said, as she began to stroll among the tables. "We spend about six weeks here each year working at the Institute, and the rest of the year we devote to our own enterprise called The Good Connection, which we started just a couple of years ago. I'm sure you'll agree that everyone needs to feel a connection of some kind. In many ways our society is more isolated than ever in its ever-increasing technological connectedness. Ever been in a store and thought the person next to you was talking to you, only to find out they were talking into a blue tooth?"

The audience winced and nodded in agreement, so Alicia continued.

"So, on one hand technology has produced instant communication with someone on the other side of the world, yes intercontinental connectedness, but at the same time it has induced local loneliness, one might say."

"That's exactly right!" a voice from a distant table called out, so Alicia invited the speaker to stand, while Kyle took her a microphone.

"Thank you for the mike, and I'm Astrid Biel. People sometimes think that those in scientific research, like me, are cold and clinical, but that's far from the truth. We need connectivity and comfort too. Loneliness has become such a social issue that recently Dr. Sanjay Gupta, Oprah Winfrey and Gayle King launched a 'Just Say Hello' campaign. They believe even such a small act of communication like that could save a life."

"Isn't that a little extreme? Can't blame technology for stuff like that," a gruff male voice called out.

Astrid was not to be dissuaded however. "Whether it's technology or just the busyness of these times the result is the same, and loneliness is a problem. So much information comes to us all the time through the media that it's hard to tell what is meaningful or important anymore. I think that's the vacuum we're facing, one of meaning in our lives. But I can tell you this, that even a wave of the hand could make all the difference. I know because it did that for me when my husband passed on recently.

"One night I was coming back to my dark apartment with such a heavy heart, when I saw light streaming out through my neighbor's door, and saw a young man there sitting on his sofa. He heard me, looked out and waved. I felt sure he was trying to comfort me and he did. But later I found out he didn't even know about my husband. So, it's not even 'just say hello,' but maybe it's 'just wave' that could be enough of a communication to comfort another. A little kindness can go such a long way."

With that comment, Astrid handed the microphone back and Alicia continued.

"Oh, yes, we here at the Institute also believe that's true, Astrid. Thanks for sharing, and I hope things are better for you now. Now, to wrap up this point, we see people walking around trying to find *a* good connection for their devices when what we really need is *the* good connection. Most of us usually set good goals for ourselves, but how many of us have goodness as the goal? So, to us, the first connection is to goodness itself and then to each other. We try to promote both ideas in our work. Kyle, you want to take it from here?"

"Sure will," said Kyle from the other side of the dining room. "So many people come up with great ideas to share and of course they do that on the web, but we wanted to provide channels for those ideas, so they could reach others in a position of implementing them. For instance, we have channels through which we could share what was brought up this morning by Josh Hamilton. The era concept would be hugely beneficial to certain government agencies and the military too. We've forged connections through which to float ideas like that. The motive can't be commercial, though of course the individual may end up writing a book, for instance. Yes, they may receive income from the idea eventually, but that isn't the motive. Just sharing good ideas with others is. It's an altruistic endeavor."

"Is this a kind of 'freely ye have received, freely give' type of thing? I mean it's in line with the Bible?" Someone near Kyle asked this question.

"Absolutely, it is." Kyle replied. The Bible is called the Good Book for a reason. Alicia and I figured it's because the goal of goodness shows up as a constant thread all throughout the Bible. Yes, did the lady at the table on the side of the room want to comment? Just a minute, let me bring my mike to you." Kyle scooted around a couple of tables until he reached hers. He offered her the microphone which she accepted, while clearing her throat to speak.

"I'd like to say I'm so in favor of what you are doing. I'm Janice Sanchez, and I work as a caregiver in the assisted living and medical field. It's so obvious to me that we can't live without goodness, yet somehow it's reserved for the young when we try to teach children to be good, or even animals to behave. We'll say to a child, 'oh, you're being so good' and to a dog, 'good boy.' But later on how many consider goodness as a goal or even an asset?

"However, when all the wear and tear and competition of this life is over and done, and you're caring for the elderly as I do, then goodness is front and center again. And why is that? Because that's all the elderly truly care about at that point in their lives. They care about kindness, and ways it is expressed to them. I've even seen people take up religion at the very end of their life as a type of insurance policy. They want to go out on a good note.

"So that's my point. Surely goodness can't just be our entrance and our exit strategies onto and off the human scene or stage as Shakespeare calls it. Pastors are right to promote goodness as a goal. But it shouldn't have any threat attached to it. I don't believe God is a type of Santa Claus who knows if you've been bad or good. And even that Christmas song ends with, 'so be good for goodness' sake.' Yes, we should be good just for the sake of goodness. It brings happiness, which is actually linked to health some experts in my field have found. But I think there's more to it. It's almost as though there is a quiet song being sung to us that's calling us all home to goodness. Guess that's all I wanted to talk about. Thanks for the mike."

"That's a perfect way of saying what we intended to, so we may as well tear up our scripts, Alicia." Kyle looked across the room to his wife and smiled. "Now, our contribution to . . ."

He was suddenly interrupted by an eager voice saying, "I have something to add to that." A man seated at the same table as Janice motioned to Kyle who immediately walked around to him.

"Yes, sure, what would you like to add?"

"I only just found out about this, but there's a bunch of people out there who talk about being good. They say they're good people, good parents and good citizens, but they don't believe in God. They have large meetings, kind of like a church with singing and inspirational speeches. If you look it up under Atheist Mega Churches you'll find it on the web. I think this movement began in England, but it's across our country and in Australia too."

"Huh, that's kind of surprising! So, they want connectivity, community and goodness. Isn't that another example then of how people today are really yearning for the good connection. Those people have banded together as atheists to accomplish it. Maybe it's their answer to goodness outside of the religious scene. So, is this the scientific era's alternative to religion? Or is it simply part of humanity's ongoing search for happiness and goodness? Wow! That's a discussion for another time, I believe."

Kyle was about to proceed when he was again interrupted, and this time by a very young man with a crew cut.

"Hey, I have a thought for you. I love looking up origins and roots of words. It was a real surprise to me that the word 'good' has its origin from the term 'god' in many of the Anglo-Saxon tongues. People worshipped good. That was their god. In a way those atheists agree with church folks who say that God is good. So maybe the atheist churches aren't quite as atheistic as they think."

"Well, that's an impressive idea, thank you." Kyle seemed puzzled and definitely surprised at the young man with such mature ideas.

"I was going to say a moment ago that Alicia and I have two points for this teatime talk. Oh just a moment, another hand is up. Okay, I'll be right there. Here's the mike."

"Hi again, and I'm Dave with the string theory. Now, this is what I've been thinking about the churches that are declining. I mean most of their members must be pretty sad about this. I feel sorry for them but would like to add some encouragement and say they've done a really good job."

"That's quite a statement Dave, and a comforting one too. But, why do you say that?" Kyle was intently interested.

"Because the churches, more than any other group I can think of, except for parents, have advertised for goodness. Also they've promoted the Golden Rule, and it's catching on. Just the other day I read an account of a Chinese activist who wants to bring the Golden Rule into all the areas of Chinese life and government."

"That's great news, Dave, and it is a success story for the ones that have made it their main business to promote goodness in the world. We can be grateful for their efforts because we all benefit."

Alicia added to that with this comment, "Yes, I think the success of churches has been falsely judged by the amount of members who fill the pews.

But surely the main and original aim of Christianity was not to fill pews, but to fill hearts with love and goodness, and an understanding of God. If that happens worldwide, then the church has succeeded in its mission."

"Yes, and that's exactly the kind of thing that we, Alicia and I, wanted to be affiliated with," Kyle said. "The goal of goodness is our first point at this teatime talk. A recent study on the subject judged the goodness of countries by how unselfish they were. I'm sure you all here would claim to have a good purpose, to be doing something worthwhile, and unselfish, for society. That one fact unites us."

"So, is that why we're mixed now at these tables? Is that supposed to show we're not really separated, but we're united in good purposes? Or is that reading too much into it?" Janice asked.

"I really don't know but it sounds fine to me, so let's go with it." Kyle's response brought forth a few chuckles, while the serving staff moved quietly and efficiently among the tables bringing in the different ingredients required for the Devonshire Tea. Kyle noticed the gentle activity and remarked on that to the audience.

"We're being served very well here, so let's give the staff a large 'thank you' for such a good job." A hearty round of applause followed his suggestion.

I OBJECT TO THE VERDICT!

Kyle spoke again, "Now, before the warm scones arrive, we need to address another point, one that's already been brought up by a few people including Dr. McIntire. It's the myth problem. Myths tend to separate us from goodness and worthwhile goals. We used to believe no one could run faster than the four minute mile until Roger Bannister did, or that we would die if a car went over thirty miles an hour. Then there were the ancient myths that the earth instead of the sun was the center of our system, and let's not forget the myth that the earth was flat. Olden-time sailors were scared to explore the high seas in case they'd fall off the edge of the earth at the horizon. And it wasn't all that long ago that the scientists knew for certain we couldn't travel faster than the speed of sound. And yet the sound barrier was broken. How many myths like that are barriers separating each one of us from something good we hope to attain?"

"Can you give us an example of that, Kyle?" Eric called out.

"Sure. Let's say you have vital information to share in a public forum but think you can't speak in public, not even to five people in one room. I knew a man like that, and he finally ended up giving talks to huge crowds. There were five thousand people in one crowd he faced in Central Park in New York City, and part of that large crowd was moving as he spoke. That never fazed him. He kept right on speaking to them all. But the myth he couldn't do it had to be exploded first. Some better idea broke that myth for him."

"So, you are saying not only we as a society collectively, but we as individuals need myth breakers?" Phyllis asked from her table close to Kyle.

"Yes, for sure we do."

A guest raised her hand and asked, "But isn't that just ordinary progress you're talking about or someone getting counseling or taking classes? Isn't it a bit extreme to call that man's hang-up about public speaking a myth? I've never heard personal inadequacies or fears called myths before."

Alicia was quick to answer. "No, I never did either till I heard someone explain it that way, but when you think about it, then it's really quite an accurate description. It was a myth about that man."

"Give us the definition of myth, please," someone called out.

"A myth is a traditional or legendary story about a person or an event," Kyle explained. "It may have a basis in fact or it may not. For instance, that man and his family, business associates and many others held that same opinion about him. They'd talked about it for years and believed it. He just couldn't be a public speaker and that was that! But when he broke through that barrier, there was nothing to it. That's why it fits in the myth category."

"So, there's really no horizon or limit to our capabilities, is that what you're saying?" A guest looked quite relieved at her own conclusion.

"That's the point they're making," another guest added. "I think today's myths are also often called urban legends too, aren't they? Kind of like the telephone game where the message gets passed from person to person and ends up as nonsense, completely off track. Put another way, it's just gossip."

"Good comments, thanks. Now, to consider a problem a myth is really a new way of dealing with the problem. Let's just ask a doctor here about that. Is there a doctor in the house?" The audience laughed at that so Kyle added, "Maybe this time we can talk with a specialist who doesn't mind being quizzed for a minute?"

A man stood up at a table near Alicia, who then shared her microphone with him. "I'm Colin Roush, and I specialize in cardiology."

"Ah, so you are a heart doctor or specialist."

"That's it, but you can't quiz me on matters of the heart as I'm certainly not a specialist in that. I've been married three times. But, I think I've got it right this time."

"An honest doctor, with a sense of humor too. I'm sure that helps in your work," Alicia said with a smile.

"Actually, it does! So what's the big question?"

"Well, Doctor Roush, would you tell a patient who comes to you that he just has to face reality and be sick?"

"Of course I wouldn't. I'd try to help him. I believe disease can be eradicated."

"You consider health then to be the natural state of mankind?"

"That's a tough question. Yes and no. Health isn't always evident but yes, we do attempt to normalize the body, so from that point of view health is a normal or natural state."

"So, to you heart disease could be called unnatural, and it's not permanent, not a fixture."

"That's uh, true. At least, that's how I approach all my cases, whether or not I can prove it."

"Thank you, Doctor Roush. That's a very humane approach, and I'm sure your patients appreciate it. So to recap . . ."

"I have something to add," Joseph McIntire intervened. "Speaking of heart conditions this is quite something. Some of you may have come across the story of Andy Mackie, a senior man up in Washington State. You can look this up on the web. He'd had nine heart surgeries, was expected to die and was given fifteen medications to take. Those drugs had really bad side effects, so he decided to stop taking all of them and instead used that money to buy harmonicas for children in schools. He passed on recently after thirteen years of giving away twelve thousand harmonicas and having taught so many children to play. It's an amazing and heartwarming story. Oh, sorry Alicia. I didn't want to interrupt, but that news report just came to mind. It also illustrates concerns so many of us have about the drug industry, but that's an investigation for another day."

"That was wonderful, and thank you. Well, I was about to recap by saying the medical faculty doesn't actually consider sickness or disease real in the strict sense of the word. The definition of real includes being immovable, unchangeable. If disease were real according to the definition then no one would undertake to heal it by any method, by conventional medicine, alternative medicine, natural remedies or by spiritual means."

"Do you really believe that's what the Bible is telling us?" A very intent guest asked that question.

"Yes, we do. It's obvious that Christ Jesus didn't view sickness or disease as a fixed fact. To him, humanity didn't need to be sick, sinful or dying. Those things were not necessary or natural to him at all. Other Bible characters were in the same mold too, in both the Old and New Testaments."

"Just a moment Alicia, someone is waving a hand at me?" Kyle called out to his wife. "Oh, yes Josh, did you want to add something?"

"Yes, I sure do. I have a buddy who covers the medical or health beat. He and I started to discuss what he was finding, and then I'd come across news reports in my work and began to take notice too. I wondered if there were many folks who feel like that. I mean, who don't think they have to settle for a bad medical situation just like that Andy Mackie. I even started watching for trends among them.

"Sure enough, I found that lots of people today don't even accept an unfavorable diagnosis let alone the medical verdict. Guess you could say the doctor isn't god anymore. Patients decide they will walk again after they've been told they never will, and they wake up from a coma when the verdict is against it. I've even read about instances where a person has been declared clinically dead, sometimes for a long time, and has revived. Just the other day the news carried the story of a Mississippi man who came back to life, kicking in a body bag, after being declared dead. He was at the mortuary and going to be embalmed."

"Oh, my gosh," Amanda was horrified. "What an awful experience that was! I know people who recovered like that from disease though, so I know it can happen."

"Yes, it can and does," Josh replied. "Specifically, I remember the case of a young boy, who must have been oh, only about thirteen at the time, who was told he had inoperable cancer and who simply said he didn't think the Lord was ready for him yet. He didn't die. He recovered fully. So it wasn't natural to those people to go along with what they were told. They resisted the verdicts."

"If they don't accept those verdicts, do they appeal to a higher power, do you think?" Phyllis asked.

"Some do. They appeal to a higher court you could say. They want a God-oriented or a spiritual solution, and then others just resist the verdicts on grounds of well, inhumanity, I guess is the best way to put it." Josh responded.

"What do you mean by that? They resist on grounds of inhumanity?"

"Well, Phyllis, I've thought about this quite a bit and have come to this conclusion. It seems that some patients pick up on the fact that, while their doctor may be a talented and a humane physician, the verdict itself is inhumane. It's unjust and unmerciful. So that's almost like a moral court of appeals they go to. They want a compassionate, just verdict. Oh, they may not explain it that way, but their statements and acts sure do go in that direction. They resist the unjust verdict to the hilt as the saying goes. So, whether it's a spiritual or a moral court of appeals, patients can sometimes be very successful with their own cases."

Kyle picked up with, "Josh makes some really good points. We've all read about amazing cases of recovery, so maybe it's not too much of a stretch to place disease in the myth category. To that young boy evidently the cancer was not some big real obstacle or a Goliath he had to overcome but more like a mistake, a fable that he wouldn't believe. Yes, it was more of a bubble to be burst, like David with his slingshot."

"Do you feel the three gifts or systems are part of that somehow?' Richard asked.

"Oh yes, we do, especially after hearing the discussions this morning." Kyle replied. "We have to allow for the possibility that what Jesus did was to expose and explode myths about us all in a number of areas, in all three systems. Perhaps he was showing over and over that we don't have to accept those verdicts. They're just not good enough. He raised the young girl who had died, saying she was asleep. He said and did the same with his friend Lazarus who'd been in the grave for four days. When the disciples questioned him about Lazarus being asleep, he said plainly that Lazarus was dead. So maybe he meant the young girl and Lazarus were asleep, like the rest of us, to what life really is, and that death is not part of it. Maybe he was saying we don't have to settle for all the miseries that come along."

Then Alicia, with a serious expression on her face, delivered her closing remarks. "Here are some obvious conclusions from our study and discussion of goodness, goals and myths. There are many playing fields in daily life where we interact with each other. If we consider ourselves to be sincere, courageous and dedicated players or participants, then we should aim for the goal of goodness and be willing to shatter prevailing records or myths. Yes, no matter what opposition there seems to be to prevent us from reaching our goal."

Alicia paused for a moment and then smiled. "Now, we'll leave you to concentrate on and enjoy your Devonshire Tea. It looks as though you've all been served. The warm scones have arrived."

She took her microphone back to the head table, as did Kyle, and they joined a group who looked as eager to talk as to eat. Someone was already suggesting, "Hey, goodness, goals and gossip would make a great title for a book or a chapter, don't you think?" The conversation never lagged from that point on but simply took turns, like the eras, while the afternoon repast was being happily consumed.

Session Three

Session Three

MOSES AND ALTERNATIVE ENERGY

Eric faced the assembled audience again with a smile and a question, "How did you all enjoy your Devonshire Tea?" Grateful applause, a few cheers, and some audible comments of appreciation were the responses, but then he asked a telling question.

"All three fields here have had great impact on our lives and are actually related to each other, and if that isn't totally obvious yet, then maybe it will be by the end of this conference. If not actually married then you are at least kissing cousins. However, it appears that some attendees didn't feel we were getting there fast enough, and so after our tea break we lost a few people from the science section, and a couple from the medical. Think we still have the religious section intact. Anyone want to give their reason for staying?"

"I want to see what you think is going to happen to the churches or religion in general, so I hope you'll polish up your crystal ball and let us in on the secret." Dee Copeland had obviously progressed past her concerns over gift giving and was now looking ahead at the big picture.

149

Eric became quite serious as he replied, "It may surprise you to know we don't possess a crystal ball here at the Institute, but following the thought trend is kind of like when they say in a movie, 'follow the money' because it usually discloses the plot or outcome. You're all part of this process today and been doing very well at it, I think."

"Speaking for the medical community here, if I may," Janice Sanchez added, "there's much we've been learning along the way, and I wouldn't want to miss it."

A minor round of applause was quickly followed by a woman speaking from the science section.

"I said a little at the tea break about comforting. Remember me, Astrid Biel? I want to say that not all scientists care little about religion or spiritual matters. There are a number of us who would like to probe more deeply into uh well, into a more spiritual dimension for life, but seem somehow confined by our own researches. The idea of the goal of goodness and the Golden Rule has to appeal across the board because when we hit rock bottom, and we all usually do at one point or another, there has to be a lifeline we can hold onto, and I for one can tell you that isn't going to be my microscope. Oh, by the way, I'm rather intrigued by this meeting today and thank you for it."

"And thank you, Astrid. Now, Julie, you were handed a few questions. Do you want to start off with those?"

"Sure, Eric. The first question has to do with our rather hasty conclusion during our first session regarding the eras. We surmised that this country was instrumental in bringing about the rotation of eras, or at least in making the three systems obvious. It appeared to us as though both medicine and science had been subordinate to religion throughout human history. Perhaps having come from that parent they were still the children, seen but not always heard. In fact, they were often reprimanded. Take for instance the problem Galileo had in promoting the idea that the sun, and not the earth, was the center of our celestial system."

"Oh, yeah," Alex agreed. "Isn't that just like human nature to consider itself the center of everything? Yup, it's all about me. No wonder they didn't accept Galileo, and yet he was still part of what has been termed the scientific revolution in the 1600's."

Dave immediately added, "But that revolution had serious problems because Galileo had to face the Inquisition. His ideas didn't match up with the Scriptures, or so they thought, and he was found guilty of heresy, forced to recant and spent the rest of his life under house arrest. Yes, he was severely reprimanded by the religious era, the stern parent of the day, even though he was right. So did medicine

151

and science have to wait until America was founded on principles of freedom, before they could take their proper place in the world? That was your conclusion wasn't it?"

Julie replied quickly, "Yes, it was, and we wanted to verify it, so at our break time Elle contacted someone who lives here locally in Santa Barbara. You want to tell this part, Elle?"

"Sure," Elle replied. "We call him 'the other Richard' and he's been a wonderful supporter of the Institute ever since it began, plus he's quite the expert on history."

"You collaborate with other people?" Joseph McIntire inquired. "Is that how you operate here at the Institute? It's just something I've been wondering about."

"No, not collaborate in the usual sense. We're not making metaphysical stew with a morsel from here and one from there. We here at the Institute each have our own source of inspiration, and I'll probably tell of mine later, but basically we listen for ideas and then see if they can be verified."

"So, you have kind of a revelation or breakthrough. In other words a bright idea hits you. Then you look to verify it. Is that correct?"

"Well, yes, that's pretty much it and we verify by a number of methods. People like Richard, for instance, can provide valuable input by commenting on our ideas regarding history. He's a constant reader, especially of historical material. We know someone else like that too, 'out-of-state Bob' is how we refer to him. He's a voracious reader, mostly of theological subjects, and will interface with us by pointing out a certain book, or a particular article or quote on the subject. We're very grateful for comments from good thinkers everywhere. Even if they object to what we come up with, it just makes us dig deeper."

"So what did the history expert have to say about your quick conclusion?"

"Well, Joseph, first we asked Richard if he agreed with what Ted Lampson had pointed out that the religious era had been predominant all through human history. He said it had, even during the Dark Ages. The rest of Ted's comment was so interesting and accurate about a one-time event in human history. My grandmother, for instance, was born in 1880 and grew up during the religious era. She lived through the medical era and witnessed the televised landing on the moon in 1969. By the time she passed on in 1975, the scientific period was probably well on its way to becoming the dominant era. Yes, she experienced all three eras as they changed."

"It's mind boggling. Totally awesome!" Amanda was almost at a loss for words.

"Oh, yes, how incredible is that! Too bad people didn't realize just what they were experiencing." Megan was likewise stunned as were so many others. "But what about the other question?"

"Well, we asked Richard if he agreed with our panel's quick conclusion that the founding of this country on freedom of religion and on democracy was instrumental in bringing the other two systems to the forefront. He agreed again, but qualified his answer by saying that freedom was set down as the guiding principle in the Constitution, but had to demonstrated in daily life. It was only in 1865 after the Civil War that the important freedoms of religion, speech and the press were increasingly acknowledged and practiced. You could say we're still on that path."

"So then this country really did provide the right conditions or environment for medicine and science to take their place." Dee was first elated at the discovery, then seemed almost sad as she asked the next question.

"But it seems to me that the child, medicine, turned on the parent, because as it grew up and became more powerful, medicine began to dictate to religion. So why couldn't they have all appeared as equals? Why did the three systems have to rotate and one be more prominent than the others? That can still lead to domination by one system."

"Oh my goodness, that's a question and a half," Eric said with amazement. "We'll have to think about that later. But right off the top of my head, perhaps the answer lies in some type of commonality. Maybe they just have to arrive at a unifying principle to have equality among the three. Now Julie has more written questions for us, I believe."

"Yes, the next question is a follow-up from our tea time about the churches being successful or failing. Who wrote this question, please?"

Julie looked around and, after a long pause, a woman in the religious section slowly stood up.

"Hi, and I'm Betsy Holcomb, and it's hard for me to even talk about this because it means, yes, it means oh, so very much to me." Her voice broke at this point, and it seemed as though she might not be able to continue.

"Maybe you could simply start with a small comment then," Julie kindly suggested.

"Okay, and it's just that uh, I feel we, that is the churches and religion in general are disappearing. The others here, those in medicine and science will be sailing off into the future without us."

"So, is that what bothers you the most?"

"Yes, but there's more. It's also the thought of losing everything that I can't bear."

"But if it's true that brotherly love, the idea of the Golden Rule, is being accepted by so much of the world then that's some success, isn't it? That's not losing everything." Julie seemed a little puzzled, but Betsy's next comment showed exactly what the sorrow was about.

"The young man who tried to comfort us about the churches declining was so kind, and I hope he's right, that we've done an okay job so far. But that's only part of it for me. It's not the whole picture. My little church will be closing soon and it's just, well, I can't bear to lose my friends and the church service. It's all so, so comforting to me to have that. Maybe I'm just selfish, but I can't bear to see it all go." She suddenly burst into tears and had to sit down.

At that point, Julie ran down from the platform to comfort Betsy, who was sitting in an aisle seat, and did so by kneeling down beside her and putting an arm around the woman's shoulders. Elle took over immediately at the front of the panel.

"I'm sure Betsy is not alone and that others in her section are experiencing many of the same sad feelings. Is there anything someone else can offer at this time? Oh, Alex. You have a scientific take on the subject?"

"Yes, in a way. The thing that has been nudging at me this whole day is the fact that we have all been transitioning from one stage to another. Doesn't matter which system you're talking about. The transitions are mostly due to improving thought trends, as you'd call them. We usually simply term it progress, but of course changed thinking has to come first and is behind it all. That's the wizard behind the curtain in our land of Oz."

"That's a great way of putting it, Alex, and our panel would definitely agree with you," Elle replied. "In fact, you've actually touched on an area that we'll be delving into, but how do you apply this to the churches and to those like Betsy who feel they are losing something precious to them? Some feel it's a failure on their part."

"Oh, no, it's not that at all. As the transition takes place it looks as though we're losing the last stage, but we're actually building on it to something higher and better. Perhaps the churches as we've known them are only in a transition mode and not being lost. I mean we don't mourn over the Ford Model T car though it was the first mass-produced car in 1908, not so long ago really in the big scheme of things. The folks who produced that car couldn't even dream of my job today at the Jet Propulsion Lab and what that entails.

"The Model T has made way for a rocket that takes passengers into outer space not over bumpy, unpaved roads. Talk about an evolution in transportation and all in about sixty years! So Betsy's church could be just evolving too and not disappearing. Maybe they can't foresee what the new form will look like but, if they will take heart and sail into the future, it just might be waiting for them around the bend in the next harbor."

At that comment, Betsy looked up hopefully and dried her eyes. With a warm squeeze of the hand, Julie left her side and returned to the platform.

"Thank you, Elle and Alex, too," Julie resumed as lead. "That was exactly what we all needed to hear, so we can thank Betsy for starting us off in that direction. As Elle said we'll be continuing soon on the same subject."

"You had another question that needed answering Julie, didn't you?" Eric asked.

"Oh, yes, I almost forgot. It's a thought-provoking one," Julie said. "We're being asked to discuss Moses and the three systems, but I'm not sure how it pertains." Julie looked around and asked, "Would the writer like to comment on this?"

The question was hardly out of Julie's mouth when a man stood up and thanked a nearby usher for the microphone. "My name is Sol, Solomon Rosen, and I'm in the science section because I work on and perform research in the energy field, all kinds of power, especially alternative energy. I'm working on the large solar project in the Mojave Desert right now. I wasn't going to come today but a physics buddy of mine convinced me it would be a good weekend trip for our families. Our wives are shopping in Santa Barbara at this very moment. Other members of the family have gone sailing."

Julie watched as a wave of understanding smiles and nods spread over the room. "I'm so glad you've found this purposeful at least for your families. But we're also going sailing today, down rivers of thought. And we hope you don't feel as though we're rocking your boat too much."

"It won't be rocked as long you can include Moses along the way."

"You mean only Moses?"

"Well, actually there are so many people involved, not just Moses, but also men like Elijah and

Elisha. They were my boyhood heroes, and I still look up to them though I'm no longer so orthodox in my beliefs and practices. They all contributed in their own way to the three fields you're talking about. It wasn't only Jesus. Moses is a great example of that contribution."

"Would you explain that for us, please?" Julie asked.

"Well, first of all the Ten Commandments fall into the theological and religious category. Moses prayed for Miriam who had been afflicted with leprosy, and that prayer healed her. Medical category! And then science, well, Moses also did amazing things out in the desert, just as we are attempting today with solar power. He parted the waters, received manna for the crowds to eat and water issued out of the rocks, which instances all broke laws of physics. Yes, there were almost too many works like that to mention. They would have to be cataloged in the scientific field."

"So you're saying that Moses contributed to the theological and religious, the medical or healing system, and the scientific one?" Julie asked.

"Yes, and not only Moses, but also Elijah and then Elisha had very similar experiences. All three systems can be seen in one form or another throughout history as we've already discussed."

"I really object to all of this faulty reasoning," a voice called out. "Remember me, Dan Voss, and I'm also in the science area, physics in particular.

At any rate, you've gone way off track. Why are you putting what everyone has for centuries called miracles, if they actually occurred at all, into the department of science? Tell me that, please! Oh the healing part we can sort of recognize as being related to the medical, but the science as well, come on, that's going too far!"

"Just wait a minute, Dan." Sol was quick to respond. "Let's remember the comment made by that young physics student earlier on. I think it was Dave who said there could be another dimension that we don't know about. I've often thought something like that when faced with my religious studies and my exploration into all kinds of energy sources. People like Moses and Elijah were powerful people, but why? Others in what you call the Old Testament were too. But again why and how were they powerful? This wasn't a case of sheer human charisma. No, that couldn't accomplish what they did. So, we may need to at least consider the alternative energy approach. They had access to another source of power that we can't even imagine from our perspective. That's what I'm thinking."

"So are you as a scientist going the route of a spiritual dimension, is that it?" Dan challenged him.

"I don't know what direction I'm taking at this point, and I really haven't delved deeply into what Jesus did or the works of the apostles as that study hasn't been part of my tradition. But I'm a good observer and can tell you this much, that what all three men did, Moses, Elijah and Jesus, were very alike in a way to each other. So that begs the question. If all of them and others, too, over such a span of time, hundreds of years, could be involved in or demonstrating such similar powers then there had to be a reason for this.

"Sure, we're now leaving the territory of simply special people somehow bestowed with incredible abilities, and we're not speculating on the idea of divine intervention either. It's more like mathematicians all solving similar problems with the same rule or principle. Guess that's where I'm going but don't have a clue yet as to the results of the journey. And I don't think you do either!" With that emphatic statement directed towards Dan, Sol sat down.

"Thank you gentlemen, and what you've given us is a perfect introduction to our next speaker, but first of all let me quickly recap the second session. We've covered so much ground it helps to keep our pathway clear and recognizable." Eric looked at his notes.

"Ah, yes, we started off the second session considering the history before the three gifts, which included the changing views of God throughout the Bible. Next, we explored the link between religion and medicine and then the link between religion and science. Then we discussed the temptations followed by Jesus' contribution to religion and also to the medical or healing system. And lastly, we were considering the possibility of another dimension, a scientific one, that Jesus might have entered and used.

"During our Devonshire Tea the subjects of goodness, myths and goals were commented on. Guess that's about it. Now Richard, you want to do the honors?" Eric turned to his colleague, while the audience looked around to see who would be walking up to the platform.

ENGLAND AND NEW ENGLAND

Richard began with, "It is my distinct pleasure to introduce our next speaker, a young man who, though only fifteen years old, has delved deeply into areas of interest to us today. You may have noticed him helping some of you to find your right section at the beginning of our conference. But he's not an usher, as you may have surmised, or an office boy. He's been sitting here listening in the row for special guests. So, Jonathan Kirkpatrick, would you please come up to the platform?"

The audience smiled, though with raised eyebrows, as they applauded a boy who looked as though he could still be in Junior High School. Jonathan's sandy hair showed off a neat style of crew cut, while his attire was a rather preppy looking tan pants and navy blazer. However, he sported no signature tie but simply an open-necked white shirt. Over all, he appeared to be the proverbial clean cut boy next door and the kind you'd want your daughter to meet. That is until he opened his mouth and shared his thoughts. He would have a hard time finding common ground with any teenager, as this audience would quickly discover.

Richard shook the young man's hand and asked about his background. "Jonathan, would you please tell us about your interests and where you are in your schooling?"

"Sure thing, Mr. A, but it won't take long. I've been pretty focused on math since I was about six years old. I love mathematics because it's so well, symmetrical and logical. I also learned to read young, so I've skipped a few grades and am in my junior year of college now. But I'm almost sixteen, so I'm not as young as you think."

At that, Richard burst into a hearty laugh and the audience joined him. The whole meeting had thus far run the gamut from inquiry, discovery, skepticism, puzzlement, an angry shouter, goodness and goals to a young boy who would hopefully further clarify the subject at hand. It seemed to be an almost needed comic relief that took place for a few minutes. After Richard wiped tears of mirth from his eyes, he continued.

"Ah yes, but what about sports, have you had any time for that kind of thing?"

"Uh, well, now and then I enjoy archery, because you have to be accurate. And I like the logic I can apply to golf. Oh, and I do play chess at tournament level."

"Right! Well, that's not a surprise to us, is it?" Richard's question to the audience was quickly met with some smiles but mostly shaking of heads in amazement. Then Richard asked, "And what field of study are you in?"

"I'm studying mathematics and physics, specializing in solar robotics."

"Oh, my, that's something! So Jonathan, you're going to share some insights you've gained from both mathematics and also from your research into the Bible. Would you like to begin now, but be warned this audience may have questions for you."

"No problem, Mr. A. I don't mind 'cause I ask so many questions too." Richard then took his place at the table with the other panel members, leaving Jonathan alone to face the audience.

"Hello, everyone." He paused for a moment to look around.

"Hello, Jonathan," a number of guests responded.

"Gee, I didn't think you'd answer me. That's kinda cool. Thanks. Well, guess I'd better start off talking about Sir Isaac Newton. Yes, that's the best place to start. I'd been doing pretty well at math when I was in first grade, and so they put me in special math classes from then on. When I was about eleven years old, my math teacher introduced me to Newton. Of course, I was really impressed by him, and pretty soon he became my hero. Just like other kids had Superman or Spiderman, I had Sir Isaac Newton. Even Einstein had a picture of Newton in his study. I guess you probably know that Newton was born in England in 1642 and lived until 1727, and that he was one of the most influential scientists of all time. Today, Newton and Einstein take turns at being the top scientist at different times in different polls. There's a lot written about him and on the web too, like how he explored optics, and even constructed a telescope to prove his hypotheses. Everyone here who works in the sciences would claim Newton as one of their own, isn't that right?"

"That's for sure, Jonathan. He's our hero too!" a voice called out.

"Yes, I knew he would be, but how about the folks in the religious section? Would you consider him one of yours as well?"

A thoughtful silence ensued until someone spoke out. "I don't see how we could consider him that. Or perhaps we just don't know enough about him."

"That's exactly the problem, I think. So many only know about Newton's laws of gravity, but there was another side to him. For instance, he didn't want people to think of the universe as a type of big clock, or just a mechanism because of his discoveries. Here's a Wikipedia report about Newton's idea of gravity and God. Newton said, 'Gravity explains the motions of the planets, but it cannot explain who set the planets in motion. God governs all things and knows all that is or can be done.' By the way, Wikipedia is a very helpful resource, but the site is being constantly edited to make sure it's accurate.

Good to keep that in mind when you use it and find other corroborating evidence too.

"Back to Newton again. Sure he was a mathematician and a scientist, but he was also very into religion and even alchemy. He wrote volumes on those subjects, writings that were never published. John Maynard Keynes, the economist, really admired Newton and all he thought and did. But, instead of calling Newton the first of the Age of Reason, Keynes actually called him 'the last of the magicians.' Isn't that something!"

"Why was that, Jonathan?" Megan called out.

"Yeah, I know, sounds strange, huh! Well, Newton was interested in things like alchemy, and also he tried to figure out difficult Bible passages, such as in the Book of Revelation. He hoped to find hidden messages in the Bible but never did, though he criticized a couple of what he called 'Notable Corruptions of Scripture' in a paper he wrote. That paper was published after his death. Maybe alchemy was on the occult side, but classifying Newton's interest in the Bible as being occult wasn't really accurate. I'd say he was trying to solve spiritual equations, not physical ones. He even thought God had chosen him to make certain Biblical passages plain to people." Jonathan paused.

"Maybe I'm giving too much background here, so my last point is that Newton was regarded as an unorthodox Christian in his day. He just didn't fit into the ordination requirements for the post of fellow at Trinity College, Cambridge, which included becoming an ordained priest. He side-stepped the requirements and still filled the position."

Phyllis asked, "Please explain why that was, Jonathan. Why was Newton considered unorthodox?"

"Well, Newton leaned towards being a Unitarian, that is a believer in one God, rather than a Trinitarian, which was the expected and accepted way to go. Trinitarians believed that God was three persons in one. How a scientist thought about religious matters was really important in those days, and so you can see how times have changed. That's not even a consideration with scientists and their appointment to posts or university positions today."

"Jonathan, maybe you ought to tell this audience a little about Cambridge University," Richard suggested.

"I don't know a whole lot about it, Mr. A. Could you clue us in please?"

Richard rose from his chair behind the table, and joined Jonathan.

"Well, during the time I lived in England with my folks, I learned some interesting facts about university life there. We visited Cambridge and saw a bridge over the river Cam called the Mathematical Bridge, a wooden bridge which Newton had supposedly designed without nails or screws to hold it together. But it was only a legend. An example of a myth spun out of the genius of Newton. That's just a piece of trivia I thought you might enjoy.

"At any rate, I also found out Cambridge University was founded in 1209, so it was well on its way to being five hundred years old when Newton was there. It was so interesting to visit. We had to duck down to go through doorways in the students' quarters because people were so much shorter in those days. It was a very prestigious school in Newton's time and still is today. In fact, Cambridge is one of the top five universities in the world.

"Now, there are a number of colleges in Cambridge University such as Queens College, Kings College and Trinity College, which was Newton's College. That's kind of ironic isn't it, seeing Newton wasn't a Trinitarian. But Newton, nevertheless, became a fellow which is a high position in the College. Yes, it's quite an honor to be elected a fellow. That's just an overview, but it demonstrates how highly Newton was regarded. So now tell us, Jonathan, how Newton's immersion in the Bible affected you." Richard resumed his place with the panel, while Jonathan looked at some notes he had with him on index cards.

"Yes, we're getting to the point now. But there's something I need to say first, and someone did mention this subject before but I'd like to emphasize it. Newton's main work was titled, 'Mathematical Principles of Natural Philosophy.' Natural philosophy was the term used then for the study of nature, before it morphed into being called physics. In fact, the term, *scientist,* as we know it today wasn't even used until after 1834. Now, all of that info about Newton and the Bible gave me an idea, and I wondered: What if Newton had been able to find something scientific in the Bible? That was a fantastic possibility to me, and so I figured I'd better study the Bible to see what I could find, and I researched more on Newton too.

"Here is another fact I found out about Newton's idea of God. He believed God had designed the universe along the lines of rational and universal principles which were available for all people to discover. And that these principles would allow us to do well in this life not just hope for salvation in the next life. That seemed to me to be a real scientific concept he found in the Bible. So I wanted to find universal principles in the Bible too. If Newton, the foremost mathematician and scientist was exploring the Bible because he wanted to discover the wisdom of the ancients, then there had to be something to it of a scientific nature. Now, before I go into the next logical step, are there any questions on this so far or shall I just continue?"

"Jonathan, I'd like to ask you something." Sol Rosen stood up and accepted a microphone from an usher. "It seems to me you're going in the direction I've been looking for. I mean feeling that the Bible characters we've been talking about had a principle or rules to go by, just as we do in mathematics. Obviously, Newton was exploring that idea. That would make so much sense to me because now we're entering the land of logic and not just blind faith. King David's Psalm 139, for instance, tells us about God's omnipresence and that we can't go outside of that. We'd say the same thing about math too as an ever-present principle.

"Of course, we believe and have faith in mathematics, but that's because we can prove at least part of it. We accept it by induction. In that case, faith isn't blind at all because it has some understanding to back it up. So, what if there is a science like that in the Bible that we can understand and have faith in too? Oh, we'd still have to prove it by degrees, wouldn't we, but at least it's there to be proved. What a breakthrough that would be! Is that where you went in your research, and did you make a breakthrough like that, Jonathan?"

"Yes, Mr. R. That's it! And omnipresence has a lot to do with the Holy Ghost which is also called the Holy Spirit, so I looked it up in Westminster's Bible Dictionary and here's what it says. 'The Spirit of God is the divine principle of activity everywhere at work in the world, executing the will of God.' But my breakthroughs came in little pieces, until I read another book on the subject.

"The book Ms. Gillman talked about at the beginning of the conference is a reference book and a key to the Bible. That's the one with the chapter, 'Science, Theology, Medicine' in it. If you think of the Bible like an ancient scroll or map, then it needs a key to understand or unlock it. And I found that's what Ms. Gillman's reference book has. I began to research that book a few years ago. My grandmother gave it to me for my twelfth birthday for two reasons. First of all, Aunt Lou had been healed by the ideas in that book. The family said she was at death's door when she had that healing. Strange expression, huh! But also my grandmother knew I'd be interested just because of the title. It's called, *Science and Health with Key to the Scriptures,* and it's by a woman who lived in New England, Mary Baker Eddy. And get this, it was published in 1875! That's only the next century after Newton died.

"People really were religious in those days, and the Bible was the main book in the house. I even found out that it wasn't considered respectful to place another book on top of the Bible. That's how much it was valued. And it meant a lot to little Mary Baker, even as a small child growing up on the family farm in Bow, New Hampshire. I researched and found out about her family. They were devout Christians. For instance, her Puritan ancestors were among the first settlers of New Hampshire, and she was brought up in the Puritan tradition of religion. Mary's father was quite strict, but she had a very loving mother, who encouraged Mary to rely on God's goodness to heal her.

"Mary Baker's family life; her church background; years of Bible research for healing principles; her own bad health; experimenting with homeopathy; and finally a pretty amazing healing all prepared her for the discovery of a science in the Bible. And there's one more thing. Her method of verifying her discovery was very scientific. Although she'd had that healing, she didn't rush right out to write and publish a book about it, but first of all found out how she was healed. She also healed other people, taught them to heal, and basically proved her discovery. She said she put the rules of this Science to the 'broadest, practical test.' So you see, though the discovery was made in 1866, the book wasn't published until 1875. Here's just a little bit of what she wrote in her book about her search and discovery. I put it down in my notes, oops."

Jonathan juggled papers while commenting, "It's kind of like the stages of a chemistry experiment. You go through aim, method, demonstration, result, conclusion. Oh, here it is! Just listen to this process." He now held a single index card as he quoted.

"I knew the Principle of all harmonious Mind-action to be God, and that cures were produced in primitive Christian healing by holy, uplifting faith; but I must know the Science of this healing, and I won my way to absolute conclusions through divine revelation, reason and demonstration."

Jonathan looked intently at the audience again. "Of course, the title of her book got to me right away, as my grandmother figured it would. When you think about it there are the three areas we're discussing today right in that one title. There's science and there's health and the Scriptures too.

Yes, science, theology and medicine. Now that's pretty incredible, isn't it!"

"So how did this book *Science and Health* help you Jonathan? What was the big point that stood out to you?" Sol was more than interested.

"The book convinced me that Newton was on the right track talking about principles to practice. If he'd continued, he might have caught sight of what Mary discovered. You see, her book even gives Principle, with a capital P as a synonym for God, along with others you can find in the Bible like Spirit, Life, Truth and Love. The more I read, the more the mystery of what were called miracles was solved. There was no supernatural power at work in the Old and New Testaments. It was a natural law of God being proved, just the same as we would with math rules and laws. This is what Mary discovered. It was a science, for sure. But it was a spiritual, divine Science. Specifically, she called it the Science of Christianity or Christian Science because it was compassionate, and would help in any human situation. Jesus proved that all the time. Would you talk about that for a minute please, Ms. Gillman?"

"Yes, but only for a minute, as we still have much on the agenda to cover. I've used the book *Science and Health with Key to the Scriptures* basically all my life, and it is a wonderful way to unlock the Scriptures. That's why I've so often thought of it as the Key book and discussed it with Jonathan that way too. Oh, we met at a conference a couple of years ago and compared notes on the subject. I loved hearing about the healing of Aunt Lou because so many of my family were healed also. Countless people all over the world have found healing to be possible by understanding God better and our own true spiritual nature as His beloved children."

"Maybe you ought to tell our audience the basis of the spiritual healing in that book, Elle," Richard suggested.

"Oh yes. It has to do with the divine Mind, God, and not the human mind. Here's what she wrote about the cause of disease. 'We should understand that the cause of disease obtains in the mortal human mind, and its cure comes from the immortal divine Mind. We should prevent the images of disease from taking form in thought, and we should efface the outlines of disease already formulated in the minds of mortals.'

"You see Mary Baker Eddy found out that disease has a mental nature and basis, and so what she discovered was not a physical, but a metaphysical system of treating disease. That's how she described it. Obviously, if disease has a mental root or cause, then it needs to be treated mentally. But the surprising thing is that her discovery covered all three systems. It certainly fell into the theological category as God is the Principle involved in this spiritual Science and the effect of it was healing. Yes, all three systems of science, theology and medicine were included in the discovery, and rather fittingly too in the title of her book." Elle paused and said, "I'll hand this dialogue back to you now, Jonathan."

"Okay and thanks, Ms. Gillman. Can you see it now, everyone? Can you imagine how excited I was to find this out, that there is a science in the Bible! It still gives me goose bumps to think about it. I just loved the logic of it all and couldn't find any holes in it. But there are some pretty big premises to agree with if you go in that direction. There's a new principle to be accepted, a divine Principle.

"Oh, and there was another book too, a modern allegory about numbers that helped me. It showed that the math on the chalkboard, which is sort of like our human lives, could often be wrong but the true invisible math, governed by a perfect principle is always correct. I'm sure we'll talk about it more tomorrow. I think my time is up now, isn't it?"

Jonathan turned to Eric who replied, "Well it's not so much a matter of time, as it is subject. We're arriving now at two themes. One has to do with the principle or set of rules the three systems are working with, and the other has to do with the mind, with thinking and its effects. We'll need to explore both to come to our point of convergence. This can be a bit tricky so please bear with us as we chart some unexplored territory together. I'm going to ask Richard to start us off with what medicine and the physical sciences have in common."

THE PINOCCHIO PROBLEM

Richard remained seated with the panel as he took up his microphone. "Well, let's see how we should begin. Basically, medical science and the other physical sciences share something in common, when we are speaking of a principle. Physical means that which pertains to a body or generally to what is material. It is separate from the mind or spirit. Yes, medicine and science share the same principle, being based on matter and the same material and physical laws. But in one case those laws apply to doctoring the body, and in the other case to investigating and working with all material objects, nature, and the universe in general. Same principle involved. Oh, did you have a question or comment, Dee?"

"That could be like an umbrella you use for the sun or for the rain. Same umbrella, but the application or use of it is different. Is that what you mean?" Dee asked.

"Uh, yes, I guess," replied Richard looking a little nonplussed. "I suppose that analogy works."

"Or else you could say it's like Pinocchio," Amanda suggested.

"What do you mean like Pinocchio?" Richard was now even more puzzled.

"Well, Pinocchio was a marionette, a boy on strings. He was made of wood, made of matter, so material and physical laws applied to him. Next, he became a living boy with a body, so you see then medical science could be interested in him at that point but not before."

"She's doing it again," whispered Richard to Eric. "I still don't see how she gets there, but she does."

Bob van Dyke entered the discussion picking up on the Pinocchio example.

"Okay, so the material, physical laws apply to Pinocchio as wood, and the physical, medical law applies to him as a person. It's basically the same law or principle, but it's just a different branch or application. Medical science has to share with the other physical sciences as it doesn't have a principle of its own to operate by. Oh, no pun intended with the word operate!"

By this time, most everyone was either laughing or very amused.

"So, what about religion? It doesn't share that same umbrella, does it?" Janice's query had the effect of replacing the smiles with raised eyebrows.

Elle responded quickly. "Well, that all depends on your idea of creation and of God, and whether your concepts are matter based, like physics, or based on Spirit."

"Could you explain that statement, please?" Janice was still intent on solving religion's role.

Elle turned to the panel and quietly asked, "If we are going in that direction, then we'll need to talk about the first and second chapters of Genesis, won't we? I mean, we did discuss this before. Religion is not like the physical sciences with their one common platform. Religion has two possibilities to consider. Is this the time to talk about it?"

The panel all conferred for a moment and came back with nods of agreement.

"Okay then," Elle said as she took a deep breath and faced the audience again. "A number of Bible scholars see a distinct difference in the first two chapters of Genesis. The first account of creation is of man made in the image and likeness of God. The verse stating that adds 'male and female' created He them.' So man and woman enter this picture together. The second account is of man, not in the image of God, but made from the dust of the ground with life breathed into him and woman created later on to help him. They really are different accounts of creation. However, they do seem to have been melded together by the time chapter five in Genesis opens. Religions over centuries have likewise blended the accounts, but they were distinct to begin with."

"Oh the second one, that's just like Pinocchio, isn't it! He started off as wood, that's like dust, and then he became a flesh and blood boy." Amanda was still delighted with her analogy, but not everyone in the religious section shared her sentiments.

"There are a number of ways we could look at that, Amanda," Pastor Candice replied cautiously.

"I heard someone interviewed recently, and he made the same comment. Yes, he said that both accounts differ. However, our congregation hasn't voiced any questions on the subject, which is probably why we haven't tackled it," Stanley Hodgson added.

Bob van Dyke asked a direct question. "Well, then Elle, do tell us what the Key book says. I know a couple of pastors who have argued this point, but not come to any strong resolution. Did that woman?"

"Oh, yes, she did. In discovering the divine Science in the Bible, she saw that the scientific interpretation of Scripture had to begin with Genesis. Her discovery rests entirely on the basis of the first account, the first chapter, as being a spiritual and not a material creation. Made in God's likeness, creation must be spiritual because God is Spirit, is how Mary Baker Eddy reasoned. So everything from there on out in this Science is based on that one fact. She never deviates from that premise. She saw the second chapter of Genesis as an allegory depicting the human, mortal condition. Guess you could say she applies the spiritual medicine of the first account to cure the ills of the second account. It's rather like applying the invisible math to correct the mistakes we make on the chalkboard, where the numerals are made of chalkdust."

"That's a rather demeaning analogy, isn't it? I'm not sure I agree with such a low opinion of human life." A member of the religious section was offended.

"Well, the Bible says it, a man made of the dust of the ground. Maybe there's something to figure out there! The symbolism it too strong to refute." Dave was not unsympathetic, but his scientific reasoning was kicking in.

"Our world or society in general doesn't really support that spiritual basis, does it?" Dee avoided the conflict but was shaking her head, almost in sorrow.

"No, it doesn't Dee, but it makes so much sense. The Bible becomes truly practical because our lives can change, if we change our basis of thinking about life," Elle replied.

"You mentioned about the invisible math, and this is starting to make some sense to me too," said Bob. "We don't view chalk numbers on a chalkboard as reality, just symbols that often can go wrong, but are corrected by knowing the math facts. We usually have in the back of our minds that the invisible math is correct and perfect. Yes, we accept that as our basis for mathematics. That would be analogous to accepting the first account of creation in Genesis, wouldn't it! So, that would mean the invisible or spiritual creation is the real one." The audience looked skeptical at that statement, then a hand was raised.

"So, if that's true, then we're being asked to look at a reality we can't see! You know the saying, 'let's face reality,' but in this case how do we do that?" Janice was extremely puzzled, but Elle answered her quickly.

"We need to look through different lenses, through a spiritual not a material sense of things. The spiritual senses show a better picture, and what's more, we are able to prove in many ways, by healing and more harmony in our lives, that this is the true view."

"That's sounds like the color blind test they gave us in a psychology class in college. If you're color blind you see one word, and if you're not, you see a different word. It's the same page and design. There are not two pages, but two different views of the same page. Is this what you mean?" Dave asked.

"Yes, Dave, that's exactly how I understand it. There's only one true creation, so how it is viewed would be the question, and that view, spiritual or material, would also determine our life experience." Elle replied.

"What does all of this involve, Elle? I mean this looking through spiritual sense to see reality." Janice was still puzzled.

"There's an exact answer to that question in *Science and Health*, and I'll find it for you." Elle opened the book at a bookmarked page, "Oh here it is. It's like going up a little ladder of thinking, and I'm sure most here have already done this.

Here's the ladder, I mean the quote. 'Spiritual sense, contradicting the material senses, involves intuition, hope, faith, understanding, fruition, reality.' I believe people use that ladder without knowing they are doing it. We were talking at tea about resisting a bad verdict. That means going against or contradicting what the material senses are telling us. Maybe folks don't even acknowledge a spiritual basis in their lives, and yet denying the evidence of the material senses, and expecting a better outcome, puts us automatically in the mode of using our spiritual sense. It can even put us on the first step of the ladder. That's what makes for heroes and medal winners. It happens all the time."

Richard spoke up. "I have an example of that. We referred earlier to 'out-of-state Bob,' the man we hear from now and then with suggestions of books to read. Well, he's a decorated Vietnam vet who served two tours over there. One time his plane was shot down, and the pilot didn't survive, but Bob did. He was now alone in hostile territory. Instead of making his way downhill as they'd been taught, he obeyed his intuition and went uphill. He told us that the intuition was strong enough to be called a 'silent voice.' He came to a clearing that proved to be the only place anywhere nearby where he could be spotted from the air. However, the clearing was too small and steep for the rescue helicopter to land, so they lowered a rope to which he tied himself. They then pulled him through the branches and flew with him until they could lower him, still dangling from the rope, onto a road. The helicopter hovered until he untied himself, then moved aside, landed and took Bob on board."

"What an experience, like a scene in a movie. And what a great intuition that was!" Megan was in awe.

"That man sure listened to his intuition and didn't go along with what looked like a hopeless situation. Guess he went up that ladder from intuition to hope and maybe further to faith. Speaking of that, did anyone in this audience hear about a gal called Janine Shepherd who was hit by a truck or van while training on a bike ride for the Olympics in the Blue Mountains outside of Sydney?"

The audience turned to look at Betsy who was so eager to share that she didn't wait for an answer to her question. "It was on YouTube. What an incredible story. You should look it up if it's still there. This young woman was a physical mess, but she didn't lose her spirit. She figured if she couldn't run or ski anymore, or even walk well, then she'd learn to fly and she did. Yes, even became an instructor. She finished a talk she was giving by saying that she wasn't her body and telling her audience that they weren't their bodies either. Obviously, she denied what the material senses were telling her and how hopeless her situation was. She even saw beyond that physical body to marvelous possibilities. I guess Elle would describe that as looking beyond the chalk on the chalkboard. And is that what you meant Josh when you talked about a court of appeals?"

"Yes, pretty much, I think." Josh nodded. "It's often just intuitive to choose the better verdict and not believe all the evidence that looks stacked up against you."

"Yes, there have been so many inspiring accounts of our spiritual sense winning out over our material sense of life. So now, this brings us back to religion again," Elle paused then asked a question.

"What is the basis for the religious system today? It's very difficult to make a strong case for spirituality and spiritual laws while resting one's plea on the second chapter of Genesis, on the material account. In fact, when you think about it, healing by pure faith is quite a monumental occurrence, if faith starts from that material basis. It has to mean that faith in the spiritual side totally outweighs the matter basis."

"What's the alternative then, Elle?" Dee asked.

"Well, if one begins with the spiritual account and considers that to be the reality of us, rather like the invisible numbers that are always perfect, then it's possible to cancel out the human mistakes about life and health, just as you would cancel out mistakes on a chalkboard. That's the simplest answer I can give you right now. And the Key book states that Jesus viewed all creation that way, as spiritually perfect, so this true view could immediately correct the errors or mistakes on the human scene."

"That's really something, and kind of hard to get around, but I sort of see what you're saying," Dave added. So, that's why it's called a science, or the Science of Christianity, because it operates on a principle, the principle of perfection. But what about the religious field in general? I don't think they start from the idea of perfection as the reality."

Elle agreed. "To be perfectly honest, most religions do not differ from medicine and science in regard to a material basis. They differ in what they preach or advocate. Religion speaks of moral and spiritual, divine laws, while the medical and physical sciences discuss material and physical laws. "

"Let's get back to the main point now," Eric urged, "because we're on the cusp of discovery. Richard began with the idea that medical and physical science share the same basic principle, that of physics, and they contain physical, material and medical laws. They are quite consistent in their basis and the laws they abide by. On the other hand, religion for the main part, has argued for moral and spiritual commandments and laws while basing its argument on the material side, the man-from-the-dust account of creation. So, there's an inconsistency there which separates it from the other systems of science and medicine."

"Then what do we draw from all of that?" Dee asked.

"We draw a very simple conclusion, but first, let's remember we started off this conference looking for past similarities, a like background, among your three systems. We even suggested we would find later a point of agreement or convergence again among you. So we are now eliminating the candidates for that convergence."

"Oh, so your simple conclusion is that the point of convergence for the three is not going to found in the laws that they each espouse." Bob van Dyke arrived quite quickly, while others were still shaking their heads in puzzlement.

"That's quite right." Eric was in agreement with Bob's statement. "Religion talks about God's laws not physical laws. So the three systems are not converging in that regard. The other candidate for convergence almost came up some time ago. Do you recall when we asked for someone to make a bridge for the three systems, and Dr. McIntire talked about his practice of holistic medicine?"

"Yes, I remember that well." Dave offered. "It stuck with me because it sounded as though medicine and even science could be going in a different direction to do with thinking."

"Exactly," said Eric. "So, from this point on we'll concentrate on thought itself as the possible point of convergence. Let's tackle it after a short standing break."

As everyone stood up, Josh turned quickly to Katie with a decision. "I don't think I should leave early in the morning, after all. I'd like to stay for the morning session, if you don't mind."

"Of course, you're welcome to stay for it. We just didn't think you'd want to report on a meeting mostly for the religious section. But anyone who has an interest should attend the morning meeting. Yes, we'd be happy to have you."

Katie was rather pleased at the prospect of having Josh stay longer. He had, over a very short period of time, become more of a friend than an assignment.

"Thanks," Josh looked at her with appreciation. "Maybe it's only an intuition, but I do have a feeling this is all too important to miss."

"Then you don't have to get back to family or anything?" Katie tried to disguise her interest as a casual question. "You talked about your brother-in-law."

"Oh, you mean Philip? He's my sister's husband. I'm more like Pinocchio with the strings off. I'm unattached right now."

"I see." Katie smiled and looked away. "You can come and go as you please then."

"Yes, and right now I please to stay." Josh looked away too, reminding himself that his focus needed to be clear and sharp, at least for the next day or so.

BEHIND THE CURTAIN

Eric tapped his microphone to get everyone's attention. "If you will all just take your seats again please, we can finish up here soon. You were promised a 4:30 closing time, but we'll obviously be about thirty minutes late. If some of you need to leave now, we'll understand," he said kindly. Then as a number of attendees got up to leave, Eric quickly added, "However, we'll be exploring the congruence or convergence of all three disciplines in these last minutes. Just as in ancient times, we believe the three systems are coming together once more, and it's due to what's behind the curtain."

That did it for those preparing to leave, and they sat down again. A couple of people called out their regrets, as they had a plane to catch, but asked for email notes on the final comments. As an usher took down their information, the rest of the participants looked expectantly at the panel.

"We'll dive right into it. No time for a lot of extraneous palaver," said Eric as he picked up and looked at some papers from the table.

"Ah ha, he's getting on his horse and riding," Josh whispered into Katie's ear. She simply gave him a playful nudge with her elbow but didn't look at him. It was too easy for her to tip over into giggles when she became tired. Some decorum was still needed she reminded herself as Eric continued speaking.

"Behind the curtain was how Alex Crandall explained the reason for transitions and progress. He said that thinking was the wizard behind the curtain in our Land of Oz, and he was so right. Of course, not every new thought trend, mode or invention is useful and good, and those that aren't usually drop away in favor of the better ideas. However, at the basis of everything is the thought process. It's thinking that propels us forward or holds us back.

"But here's a surprising departure even for us at the Thought Trend Institute. As we explored our topic about the churches and the three systems, something finally became crystal clear. We needed to drop the word '*Trend*,' and just look at '*Thought*' itself. Yes, thinking became the subject and this became the question. How does our thinking change our bodies, our lives and our universe? And then the next question logically followed. What does each of the three systems have to say about this? Now, our committee has done some digging to uncover answers in science, theology and medicine, but we welcome your input as always. Okay, Richard, what do you have for us?"

Eric turned the meeting over to his colleague, who didn't waste time in the shallows but dove right into the deep.

"First of all, I need to make clear that the terms, quantum physics, quantum theory, and quantum mechanics are often used interchangeably."

Some of those sitting in the religious and medical sections looked rather doubtful regarding that clarity, but Richard didn't take note of their reaction and so continued.

"Now, the current and growing trend is to allow for the fact that thinking can change everything, from our health to our everyday life and even the universe itself. Here's something I copied from the website of Dr. Milo Wolff, a mathematical physicist, regarding the quantum universe. He was asked the question, 'What is Space Resonance' and here's his answer." Richard quoted the website with gusto.

"It's my new mathematics of the structure of matter, proposed by Erwin Schrödinger that empty space can propagate quantum waves travelling with the speed of light. Elementary particles, such as electrons, protons, are made of spherical standing wave patterns, a Space Resonance, similar to the waves on a drumhead or a string. That is, all the matter in the Universe is made of waves in empty space and nothing more! All the 'material' properties of matter and its 'fields' are only schaumkommen (Schroedinger's words)— they're only appearances."

The reaction from the major part of the audience could only be described as a collective "huh?" followed by a remark from the science section.

"Yes, it's good to be shocked. Niels Bohr, the quantum physicist, said, 'If quantum mechanics hasn't profoundly shocked you then you haven't understood it yet.' And here's another quote from him. 'Everything we call real is made of things that cannot be regarded as real.' That's right in line with the Milo Wolff statement Richard just quoted."

Someone from the religious section objected. "It you don't want this meeting to end on a note of total bewilderment and ambiguity, perhaps you'd better begin with smaller steps or else explain more."

"Oh, sorry, old boy," Richard immediately apologized. Guess I did dive into the deep end of the thinking pool. Uh huh, well, yes, it took me awhile of wading in gently to get there myself. Basically quantum physics is challenging the nature of matter and the material world. Certainly Dr. Milo Wolff is in his statement. He's saying, at least this is my take on it, that what we see and call material things are not substantial at all, just appearances. It has all to do with what we think. We are viewing thought itself. Seems he is going in a completely metaphysical direction, and so are many others like him."

"That's the direction, yes," Eric added. But could we really call it completely metaphysical? I mean he still has his feet firmly planted on protons. While matter is in the mix, it would have to be a semi-metaphysical direction, wouldn't it?"

"Oh, yes, I see what you mean, Eric. Of course, you're right. It's a semi-metaphysical direction," Richard quickly replied.

"You're both still in the deep end, and I'm either completely or semi lost. So, could you back up a little more please? Or maybe tackle it from a different perspective?" Megan waved her hand as she asked.

Eric made a suggestion. "Yes, maybe we should look at this through the eyes of another system to begin with. Quantum physics may not be everyone's cup or tea."

"That's for sure!" was one immediate comment while others murmured their assent.

"So why did you start with it?" another voice queried.

Eric answered, "Because this concept regarding the illusory nature of matter and the place of mentality exists to some degree in each of your three systems at this point in time, though perhaps it's a fact that has not been generally recognized. Are you all surprised by that?"

Eric surveyed the audience, which returned a decidedly "yes" vote to his question, so he continued.

"It appears that a major convergence of all three systems could be taking place, with all meeting at the corner of thought. But we'll leave physics for a moment and explore elsewhere."

Eric's statement was met with some concern from the science section. "I hope you'll return to the science field soon because it's really important for everyone here to understand the contributions to our world made by the sciences, physics in particular." Dan Voss was strong in support of his field.

"You folks there in the religious section ought to figure out how to tie up with us in the sciences. Just look at how we've helped the medical field with life-saving inventions and our technology. If it were not for physics there would be no medical technology. For instance, the MRI machine is based on advanced physics' principles. It's obvious the medical field certainly has benefited. Let's face it, the medical system is out of its era too, and maybe that's why alternative medicine has sprung up. But we in the sciences have taken them under our wing. I suppose you could say they are still sharing our umbrella."

At that comment many in the medical section looked over at Dan and glared, while he continued on with his final statement. "Yes, just look at what physics has accomplished in so many ways."

"True, and look what you've brought upon us in other ways," suggested Stanley Hodgson.

"What do you mean by that?" It was Dan's turn to glare, and this time at Stan, who stood up to face the audience.

"It's obvious when you really think about it, with *think* being the operative term here. Physics relates to physical and physicality. So maybe we should credit you with the physical fitness craze and the rise of the gym during your reign as top dog. And then during the same period we've been introduced to action filled movies full of physical force, plus violent video games, not to mention the despicable practice of and rise in bullying, which is basically physical and or psychical control over another human being. Yes, perhaps we have a lot to thank you for." Stan sat down again having delivered his rather eloquent but startling statement.

"Hullo, hold on a minute there. What about your fear-raising tactics to do with being saved, or being otherwise disposed of! You've brought about a bunch of neuroses due to those fears, haven't you? We could thank you for that, as well as your attempts to promote goodness, which uh, of course, I'm in favor of."

The audience and panel were stunned into silence at the exchange, then Stan spoke again.

"Oh, my, just listen to us. This is awful. I'm so sorry, and of course you're right, Dan, in your comments which just point up the fact that there are pluses and minuses to all human actions and beliefs. The human kingdom is full of contradictions, of both good and evil. I'd point to another kingdom for investigation. At any rate, Dan, please accept my apology."

Dan was silent for a moment and then rose to the occasion, but not to his feet. He remained, with arms crossed, sitting stoically still and almost muttered, "Well, uh-huh, I do understand where you're coming from, and agree about the pluses and minuses. How to find the plus side only would be of great benefit to us all."

"Wouldn't the plus side only be like well, like heaven on earth? I think we all use that saying in each of our systems, don't we? We have that in common." Amanda's youthful, innocent comment was met with relief, smiles and some applause.

"Good point Amanda," Eric agreed. "So, let's all plunge right into another field. Julie, would you tackle that same question, about mentality and matter, but in the medical system? You've come from that field, so you're well qualified to comment on it."

"It's nice of you to say that, Eric, but my years of hospital administration are well behind me, and many perplexing questions regarding the medical field are in front of me. So, please don't think me shallow, but that's the end of the pool I'm headed towards."

"Good, let's go there," someone called out. Feeling the approval of the audience, Julie smiled and continued with an admission.

"I'd always looked rather narrowly or even suspiciously at Voltaire's statement that the art of medicine consists in amusing the patient while nature cures the disease, but some time ago I began to wonder if he was more on target than we know. There are so many accounts of people investigating the concept that thinking changes everything, from our relationships to our health and even our universe, that they are too numerous to mention. We here at the Institute have been taking note of the trend.

"Just recently I watched part of a PBS program, 'Mind over Medicine' with a young woman doctor, Lissa Rankin. She took the side of thinking and its effects on our health. She discussed placebos and mentality, and even ended up by suggesting it would be a good idea to heal the medical health system. Now, that's quite a challenge, isn't it! And it's one that wouldn't have been voiced a few decades ago. Perhaps society today would ascribe these forays into the effect thinking has as fringe investigations. However, what is far out today could easily become mainstream by tomorrow."

Ian Flinders, the pre-med student seemed intent on backing Julie up on the medical side because he immediately added, "I've been looking into the same thing, I mean about the place of thinking in our lives. You only have to go on the web and enter words like, 'change your thinking, change your life' and so many supporters of that come up in the religious but also the medical field. Yes, there are many promoting the same idea."

Then the science section took hold as Kristin Turner stood up.

"Well, I've seen a number of programs too, such as one called 'Super Brain' with Dr. Tenzi. He and Deepok Chopra have co-authored some books and CDs on the subject. The statement that stopped me in my tracks was something like this. He said we've all heard about 'mind over matter' and now we should be thinking about 'mind over brain.' So, isn't he also saying that thinking has the power over the body? He must be. He made a distinction between the two, between mind and brain. I don't recall hearing much about that before."

"Oh, I have." Joe McIntire brought the discussion back into solely the medical system. "That distinction is in the Larry Dossey book, *Reinventing Medicine,* where he discusses nonlocal mind as he calls it. I mentioned it earlier, but we didn't take time to discuss it. The mind is no longer confined to the body. He wrote that a decade ago. Dossey has concluded there are three eras of medicine. First, was the basically physical-only side where the patient was, excuse the mental picture of this . . . more or less just a piece of meat to be inspected. It was popular for such a long time. Then next came the mind-body era of medicine, which finally attained some status in the medical community. The patient had thinking attached to the body."

"So, it was a thinking piece of meat now?" Dave's quick comment brought forth some laughter.

"Very funny, Dave, but in a way, yes, and it was an advance for the medical field. However, this progress was frowned on in the early days as being too far out there and almost heresy to traditional medical beliefs. I had to endure peer disdain and disapproval years ago when I began the practice of holistic medicine. But there's one more step according to Dossey. He proposed we are entering the third era of medicine which he calls nonlocal.

That's the idea of a mind that can go beyond both the brain and body."

"Well then, he agrees with Milo Wolff and with Dr. Tenzi and Deepok Chopra, and the woman doctor, Rankin, on TV, doesn't he!" exclaimed Dave. "We have medicine and science agreeing on the basis of what thinking does and a mind that is superior to both the body and the brain."

Richard re-entered the conversation. "Perhaps we can go back now to physics and the point that was made about the insubstantial nature of matter. It was viewed basically as a thing of thought, an illusion, and in the larger sense ultimately unreal."

"Is it possible that perhaps Jesus was actually trying to teach us, by his words or acts, that matter is unreal? I mean he spat on the ground, which was a sign of contempt." Betsy added.

"Good point," replied Julie. We should study the Bible with that question in mind. But what we do know is that both the medical and science fields are facing the variableness of material conditions. The body can lose a disease according to the thought about it. And matter can move, lose its shape, change or disappear, according to what the observer is thinking. We have to admit that's pretty strong stuff. Even the physical scientists had problems with their own discoveries, didn't they?"

"Sure they did," Dave Gardiner agreed. Newton and Einstein had a rather orderly universe somewhat like a highway with intersections and turnoffs, and all the traffic proceeded according to the rules of the road. Then guys like Max Planck, Niels Bohr and Erwin Schrödinger lifted up the hood of a car and said, 'Hey it's a total mess in here, absolute chaos with wires going everywhere and every time we touch one wire something else changes. But, we have to face facts that this is what is steering the car. This is the operating system of the micro world. It's not just a macro system after all. We have a micro world called quantum physics too. I suppose we'll have to look for a Unified Field Theory or Theory of Everything that unifies the orderly rules of the road, the macro world, with the chaotic micro quantum world of the engines.' That's about what they would have said if they'd used an analogy, I believe."

Alex nodded slowly, "Yes, that's why Einstein, though his findings advanced the field of quantum mechanics, said he couldn't believe that God would play dice with the universe. He didn't like the uncertainty factor. "

"He wasn't the only one, Alex. Even Schrödinger is reported to have said that he didn't like it, meaning the probabilities of quantum mechanics, and was sorry he ever had anything to do with it." Dave added that piece of information.

"Is that the principle of uncertainty? They were all uncertain, weren't they!" Amanda asked.

"No, Amanda," Dave was quick to reply. "The principle of uncertainty had to do with particles not people. Heisenberg, the quantum physicist formulated it. Basically it says you can't know both the position and the momentum of a particle at the same time."

"Okay, but in a way though, Amanda is right, and that does refer to people too." Janice backed up the young intern. "For instance, I know a woman named Laura who is the CEO in a care facility, and she's a whiz at renting out the rooms. She told me that she's not particularly patient and doesn't even like marketing. Just has to do it now and then when the marketing position is vacant. Then she admitted she told inquirers they really needed to be there at that place and at that time in their life. She was decisive and took the uncertainty factor out of the decision. Yes, she brought momentum and place together, and people signed up."

"Oh, I like that," remarked Betsy Holcomb. "That's what we need. I don't like feeling uncertain."

"Obviously neither did the scientists. If we can see it from their point of view, it was a huge change in physics from certainty to uncertainty, that is, from Newton to quantum." Richard added. "If any of you saw the play *Copenhagen* about an imaginary conversation between Bohr and Heisenberg, then you may have been surprised at the statement that quantum physics put man back in the center of the universe. However, if you think about it, that's quite true. Newton had God as the center of the universe, but quantum physics has man. If man's thinking changes matter, as quantum physics states, then you can see why they'd say that. Yes, Einstein talked about playing dice because he didn't like the probabilities and changeability of quantum mechanics, but preferred the certainties of the rules of the road according to Newton."

"Well, now I'm lost on the highway instead of in the deep end of the pool," said Candice. "Please tell us how this applies to everyday life."

Elle replied, "Well for one thing Einstein's proposed fourth dimension of a space-time continuum was squeezed, and probably by the new physics. Everyone was suddenly running out of space and time. The storage unit business suddenly appeared almost out of nowhere. And as for time, do I need to say more? The fast-forward generation was born, and time was in very short supply, and it still is."

"Say, Elle, you wrote a paper on that, didn't you?" Julie faced her colleague.

"Oh yes, I did, and it was a long one but maybe a couple of specific highlights would help here. Let me think about which ones I should mention."

Elle paused only a moment then continued, "Okay, let's consider the chance factor of quantum physics. Yes, Amanda was right and people as well as particles are affected. As the uncertainties of quantum physics took over in the scientific community from about 1980 onwards, then out in society we found subjects of chance taking shape too. Casinos and state lotteries sprang up and gambling became an institution. The chance of winning was so alluring. On the other hand, the chance of losing was taken note of with some concern, so insurance policies became a must even for items as small as a thirty dollar telephone. The hope of what *might* happen and the fear of what *could* happen took center stage. The chance or probability factor makes for uncertainties all across the board in daily life."

"So are you saying we should only concentrate on the certainties of Newtonian physics?" Dee was puzzled.

"Not at all," Elle replied. Those options are both simply on the chalkboard so to speak. They're like two sides of a coin, different, but it's the same coin. It's physics. If we go off the chalkboard, higher than physics into metaphysics, especially Christian metaphysics, we find other answers and even leave the uncertainties behind."

"How does that happen, Elle?" Dee asked.

"Let's add theology to the mix here, but first let's put it all in chronological order. When we were discussing what happened before the gifts were opened, we found that both the system of medicine and of science had come from religious beliefs and practices. It may be surprising but it appears this same order could be happening again today with the current interest in and even emphasis on thinking. That interest didn't begin in the twentieth century with medicine or quantum physics. Does anyone know the history of that thought trend?"

"Yes, I think I do," Astrid answered. "I was reading up on comforting ideas. You remember I mentioned about my husband passing, and I really needed comfort. I came across some nice ideas and decided to trace them back. I found out that among thinkers in our society especially on the East Coast in the 1800's, there was intense intellectual inquiry into the place of the mind and its effect on the human body and life in general. Transcendentalists like Emerson and Thoreau were also in the mix. Many ideas were developed during that period and within the context of freedom of thought and religion."

Elle agreed, "Yes, and this is where context really counts. It was in that atmosphere, that mental climate of inquiry and religion that Mary Baker Eddy made her spiritual discovery. Added to that, women like Susan B. Anthony and Elizabeth Cady Stanton were agitating for women's suffrage. The movement for female equality was on the march. You could say those times were ripe for and even supported an intellectual, scientific and religious discovery made by a woman.

"Now regarding the effect of thinking, this was a strong theme with Eddy. She wrote about the mind and the brain in many places in her book, *Science and Health.* One is short and right to the point and is being echoed today. 'Remember, brain is not mind.' She also encouraged people to guard their thinking if they wanted to rule out sickness and maintain health and harmony."

"Can you give us an exact quotation about that? It sounds like helpful advice." Astrid asked.

"I sure can, because it's something I've memorized to help me too. She wrote in her book, 'Stand porter at the door of thought. Admitting only such conclusions as you wish realized in bodily results, you will control yourself harmoniously.' Isn't that something! A woman, whom we could really call a spiritual explorer and discoverer, wrote that in a book published in the year 1875!"

"You'd better mention the spin-offs too, Elle," Eric suggested. "There was not a straight line of descent for the thought movement, as I recall."

"That's very true, Eric. I believe we'll go into more specifics tomorrow of how the thought movement developed, but for now we need to mention one fact about it. Some early pupils, who at first followed Mary Baker Eddy's discovery, moved away from the basic premise of life based on Spirit, not matter, and into the positive thinking arena. You may remember the quote I gave about the human mind or the divine Mind. Mrs. Eddy, as students of her Science often refer to her, taught reliance on a divine Principle, the divine Mind. However, the aim was not only for the healing of the body and the ills of human life, but to solve the problem of being. This involved understanding and proving what life truly is. So many who entered the thought movement concentrated only on human life with its many needs and on the human mind for solutions.

All in all, that movement, in different forms, was snowballing down through the decades and on into the 1900's when first medicine, and then quantum physics, would also join the thinking parade."

"Wow, oh wow! So, thinking really is where our three systems meet today." Amanda was thrilled with the new development.

However, an unidentified participant in the science section was almost incredulous. She added her comment, though with some agitation, "Now, let's not rush into this. If the three systems are converging and agreeing with the idea that thinking changes the universe and the body too, then aren't we on a slippery slope? Aren't we on the path to losing our faith in matter? I mean, to have matter shift around depending on thinking makes it seem pretty insubstantial doesn't it?"

"Sure does!" Dave added. "Maybe that's why quantum physicists like Schrödinger and Wolff claimed matter is basically unreal. They were actually saying how untrustworthy matter really is, which brings up the question. On what will we base our lives or investigations in the future? Where do we go from here? I guess in the final analysis the question will actually be: What shall we trust?"

"That is a momentous question," Eric said. "Let's all take a minute to ponder it." At that, Eric put down his microphone along with the rest of the panel, and the room retreated into some moments of total silence.

CLOSING WITH QUESTIONS

Eric looked serious, almost concerned, as he surveyed his audience again, knowing they were approaching the final chapter of the day. How would it be written he wondered, and would it have a happy ending? Those were the questions that plagued him the most. The intentions of the Institute were of the highest, of that he was sure. But how this exploration might be perceived was still doubtful. Would it appear as though territory was being given away or won by any special interest or era? "It all has to be kept in balance," were his final thoughts as he prepared to speak to the gathering. However, the very first question seemed aimed at throwing it all off balance.

"Why are we even talking about trust now? I want to know why you think anyone here would have an answer to that. You're turning this into a philosophical discussion. It's all totally nebulous and irrelevant." Dan Voss asked and answered his own question in a challenging manner.

At that comment, Bob van Dyke stood and requested a microphone.

"The answer to the question of trust is in the possession of every single person at this conference.

It is with them every day in tangible form. The answer is not nebulous at all. It's not hidden in a secret chamber, not esoteric, and definitely not a mystery to be solved. Every person here has the answer in their pocket or wallet, on a coin or on a bill that carries the motto, 'In God we Trust.' It's obvious, isn't it? If we can't trust matter, that recognition alone should push us into faith in the opposite direction. Yes, we should trust the opposite of matter, which is Spirit, God. It would be nice to do it without the push, but that isn't usually how it goes, is it? We find out what won't work and then opt for what does.

"The concept of trusting Spirit not matter is another thread that runs all through the Bible. It's a secret hiding in plain sight in both the Old and the New Testaments. For instance, we're constantly warned not to trust riches that fly away, and we're told that wisdom is far more precious than gold. Though usually construed as urging us to relinquish habits of acquisition or greed, there is much more to these warnings."

"I agree with Bob," Candice said. "As there is neither a poverty nor a prosperity gospel being preached in the Bible, the warnings go much deeper. We're being told over and over that Spirit is all we can rely on or trust. Paul explained to the Galatians exactly what it means to lean on the spiritual not the material. You know it by its fruits. He said, '. . .the fruit of the Spirit is love, joy, peace, longsuffering, gentleness, goodness, faith, meekness, temperance: against such there is no law.' There is no law that can rob us of spiritual things. Only the material side of things is in jeopardy. That's a fact."

"Hold on! You were talking about thinking a minute ago, and now it's all about trusting Spirit. Make up your mind! Hey, maybe you simply have both. You have a spiritual and a mental world, is that it? And are medicine and science supposed to flow naturally from your religious beliefs again? Is that where we're headed, with history repeating itself?" Dan Voss was more than a little disturbed.

Eric intervened. "Oh, no one is claiming that, though you do make an interesting observation there, which could even prove to be true."

"Well, I thought religion was all about faith, but if religion is so expert at the business of thinking too, then tell us just where it says that in the Bible!" Dan demanded an answer, and Sol quickly replied.

"I've got one for you from the wise man I was named after. Solomon in his Proverbs told us this about a man. He said, 'As he thinketh in his heart, so is he.' That's how important thinking is."

"And I have one from the New Testament. Let's take what Paul said to the Philippians." Elle opened the Bible. "I have it bookmarked. Oh here it is, 'Finally, brethren, whatsoever things are true, whatsoever things are honest, whatsoever things are just, whatsoever things are pure, whatsoever things are lovely, whatsoever things are of good report; if there be any virtue, and if there be any praise, think on these things.' So what conclusion do we draw from this?"

Betsy Holcomb had evidently lost the sad uncertainty about her church's future for she rushed in enthusiastically.

"Well, if we consider this earthly life as a classroom, and lots of people do, then we're all learning lessons. So what Paul said is like a counselor telling us what subjects to take in school. Take the important basic ones that lead to graduation. Take subjects like truth, honesty, justice, purity, loveliness, good news."

"Perfect comment, Betsy," Elle stated, "and whatever subjects we take we are liable to see examples of all around us, because we are inviting them into our lives. That's basically what the Key book says. Listen to this! 'Hold thought steadfastly to the enduring, the good, and the true, and you will bring these into your experience proportionably to their occupancy of your thoughts.' So right or good thinking, in other words choosing better subjects, does bring good results. We'll see healing of the body and of bad situations too. Yes, we'll see all kinds of change due to a change of thought or base."

"Wait just a minute," Sol was now somewhat concerned. "If we totally follow that trend then maybe you'll suggest that metaphysics should one day take the place of physics. I've been interested in a new science that might augment physics, not replace it."

"We're not suggesting, just following leads here," Eric replied quickly. "But should metaphysics one day be looked upon as most indispensable to our lives then physics would at least have to subordinate to it, wouldn't it?"

"Then the same would be true of medicine." Dr. Roush was now obviously perturbed. "Next, you'll be saying that metaphysics will be superior to or take the place of material means and medicines in the treatment of disease. I know mentality factors in, but not to that extent."

The ensuing murmurs of many attendees attested to their disquietude and concern as well.

"I think it's too early in the game to call the score. Progress is always made step by step." Julie sought to calm the waters and comfort the audience.

"We all want the same thing. We'd like to see the miseries of the world recede, and even disappear for us individually and collectively. We'd all like a little of heaven on earth. The question is how to attain that state, and if it means choosing better subjects to think about, as Paul is telling us, then why not at least look into that. Wouldn't we all be willing to think better thoughts in order to have a better world here and now?" Julie paused, looked around the room and repeated firmly, "Well, wouldn't we?"

The sparse affirmative and rather subdued comments were not left to linger alone for gradually, like a symphony building to a climax, the yeas grew louder and more frequent until a resounding "yes" filled the auditorium.

Eric then picked up his microphone and said quietly, "Speaking of trying to call the score too early in the game, you'll remember during our Devonshire Tea we talked about the goal of goodness. We are all united in this goal in one way or another. Now, what if achieving that goal produced an incredible result? Could it even bring about the end of human problems and troubles? Surely, we'd all like to see the miseries of the world recede and disappear as Julie stated. Elle says there is that kind of promise in the Key book. She's going to read it to us now. Elle, the floor is yours."

"Thank you, Eric. Yes, right in line with taking the best subjects in this earthly school, right in line with what good thinking and acting can accomplish, and right in line with our own goals, here is a beautiful idea about the kingdom of heaven which we'd all certainly welcome.

"From *Science and Health with Key to the Scriptures* by Mary Baker Eddy is this statement: 'Let unselfishness, goodness, mercy, justice, health, holiness, love—the kingdom of heaven—reign within us, and sin, disease, and death will diminish until they finally disappear.'"

"Thank you Elle," Eric turned to the audience, "And now we really need to wrap up. It's obvious, isn't it, that all three systems, those of science, theology and medicine are being faced with the possibilities of what thinking is and does. Each field will be impacted. Today we tried to keep the discussions more general, but tomorrow will be different, and specifics of thinking will be tackled along with religious concepts. In our own notes, today's conference had the working title of 'Three Gifts,' and tomorrow's meeting will be titled 'Three Gifts Forever.' That is, if it goes the way we hope and expect."

"Can you tell us what this all means and how it will affect the churches?" Candice asked hopefully, looking at Elle for answers.

"No," replied Elle. "Not just yet, but tomorrow should bring more answers. However, I can tell you this now. After all our pondering, listening for ideas and research, we here at the Institute feel that the greatest challenge is going to be to the religious field or system, especially if organized religion continues to decline. Yours is the task of finding spiritual answers and of proving that the Bible truly is practical, that its moral and spiritual precepts and inspiration are needed for our everyday lives, and for each system, regardless of era.

"The medical and scientific fields are considered by most people to be quite necessary. But can the same thing be said of religion? However, if religion is based on an understanding of God then theology becomes the vital component. One opinion on the web states that without theology religion is no longer religion. Perhaps the need right now is not so much to involve others in religion, as it is to have a theology that answers questions for us in any era. What do we understand of God? Yes, what is the theology for today, for this scientific age?"

Julie then stepped forward for her summation. "Perhaps many are unaware that hospitals are also facing closures. Medical practice is changing as we speak. Doctors are diagnosing from a distance and through electronic diagnostic methods. The change from large centralized treatment centers could continue as medical treatment in more local situations, such as nursing homes, becomes more prevalent. But no matter how or where medicine is practiced, the medical community will doubtless continue to discover they have a micro world of thought to deal with, not just a macro world of the body. This discovery could end up re-inventing medicine as Dossey suggested.

"Now, that might be just as unsettling for the medical side as the quantum leap into uncertainty or probabilities was for Einstein and Schrödinger on the science side. No matter how the context or packaging changes, all three systems are going to find themselves faced with the same issue of content, of how thinking affects everything."

Richard wrapped up with his comment on the meeting. "This is obviously no longer simply a question of the churches diminishing due to the era, but the larger picture is demanding our attention. We at the Institute look forward to seeing what or if anything comes from our meeting today that will help address that larger picture.

"A few minutes ago, someone slipped the panel a question asking if we thought the eras might revolve again, suggesting next time it would be religion accompanied by the media. That's quite a thought and not a particularly encouraging one we think. You may recall that Dee asked why the three systems could not simply co-exist as equals without rotation, not having one dominant over the others. This concept is far more appealing, I'm sure, to most of us here. And it could be that we are approaching the answer. As you each evolve along the thought path and follow it higher and higher, a new type of unity could appear, one in which you will be equals, each one necessary and equal."

As Richard stepped back, Eric came forward, turned and motioned to his panel. "So now, thanks are due the panel and to the whole committee."

He then spread his arms out towards the audience. "And thank you all for attending and contributing to this day together. It's been very special. Would those who are signed up for or wish to join in the morning meeting please gather together in the middle section and wait for a few minutes?

Now, again, we thank you all for coming and wish those who are leaving a safe journey home."

Applause came quickly on the heels of this last statement. Then for some participants it was a speedy exodus, while others took their time to mingle and to talk. Eric and the panel left the platform to shake hands, hear comments, and to make sure everyone had transportation.

The group who had signed up for the morning meeting waited patiently in the main conference room. This little assemblage was comprised mostly of the religious section but, surprisingly enough, they were joined by others from the medical and science sections too.

Joseph McIntire glanced back at the rows behind him and saw Sol Rosen sitting next to Betsy Holcomb. "We've integrated it seems," he remarked to himself, as he got up and walked towards them.

"Hi, there. Guess it won't be much longer before we hear the details of tomorrow's meeting. But you know, I was thinking of your concern, Betsy, about the others sailing into the future without you, remember?"

"Oh, yes. That seems like a long time ago, and yet it was just this afternoon. We've all traveled a distance, I suppose." Betsy smiled at Joseph, who then turned his attention to Sol.

"Well, Sol, I don't think Betsy and her church friends are going to be left behind after all. What do you think?"

Sol looked down at the floor for a moment, then looked back up and said slowly, but with conviction. "No, they won't be left behind. I think we'll all be sailing into the future together."

"Is there a reason you feel that way, Sol?"

"Yes, actually there is. Though I'm deeply immersed in the sciences, I can't ignore my early religious education and foundation. I can't believe that what Moses did was all for naught or meant to simply disappear. He did help the world align with a new North Star to travel by, as someone described it. We all need a moral compass."

Betsy looked hopeful as she asked a question. "Well, Sol, what do you think about the star of the East that the Wise men saw? Won't that factor into the future too?"

"If all those mighty men in the Scriptures used the same principle or type of science, then the star of the East would have to be part of the whole picture, wouldn't it!"

Joseph and Betsy nodded in agreement. As Joseph returned to his seat, he couldn't repress the great sense of anticipation he had, nor did he want to. He was part of a new adventure, perhaps even a new beginning. And he wasn't alone in those feelings.

Josh finished interviewing all those who were willing to share their thoughts and then joined Katie in the auditorium. He was shaking his head in amazement as he sat down beside her.

Katie looked at him inquiringly. "So what do you think? A few surprises along the way?"

"This whole conference has been surprising. I feel as though great progress has been made, but that it's a fragile conclusion we arrived at today. Yes, fragile is the only way I can explain it."

"Then, we'll just have to protect it, won't we! We'll put some kind of bubble wrap around it." Katie smiled at the mental picture she'd just painted, and so did Josh.

"That's a good idea," Josh replied lightly. Then he added very thoughtfully, "Yes, we should protect it, because our conclusions today could heavily influence tomorrow. I don't mean just our meeting tomorrow morning, but all the tomorrows. In what direction will we go?"

"You mean it's what Betsy was wondering about? Will we all sail into the future together with no one left behind?"

"Yes, that really is the question."

Katie nodded. "Maybe it's like that 60's folk song that Peter, Paul and Mary used to sing, 'The answer is blowing in the wind.' Look outside Josh. See how the wind has sprung up."

The Thought Trend Institute and its surroundings were being suddenly and completely enveloped in gusty winds. Trees were bending in a new direction. The wind had shifted. It was a good omen perhaps. Yes, tomorrow would be a different day. It just might be the perfect day for sailing.

For ordering and author information
please visit the Mountaintop website:

www.MountaintopPublishing.com